A Treasure Hunting Text

Ram Publications
Hal Dawson, Editor

Modern Metal Detectors
Comprehensive guide to all types of metal detectors; designed to increase understanding and expertise about all aspects of these electronic marvels

Gold Panning is Easy
Excellent new field guide shows the beginner exactly how to find and pan gold; follow these instructions and perform as well as any professional.

The New Successful Coin Hunting
The world's most authoritative guide to finding valuable coins, totally rewritten to include instructions for 21st Century detectors.

Treasure Recovery from Sand and Sea
Step-by-step instructions for reaching the "blanket of wealth" beneath sands nearby and under the world's waters, totally rewritten for the 90's.

Modern Electronic Prospecting
Explains in layman's terms how to use a modern detector to find gold nuggets and veins; includes instructions for panning and dredging.

Weekend Prospecting
Offers simple "how-to" instructions for enjoying holidays and vacations profitably by prospecting with metal detectors and gold pans.

Treasure Hunting Pays Off
A basic introduction to all facets of treasure hunting...the equipment, targets and terminology; totally revised for 21st Century detectors.

Buried Treasures You Can Find
Complete field guide for finding treasure; includes state-by-state listing of thousands of sites where treasure is believed to exist.

Treasure from British Waters
One of Great Britain's best known detector hobbyists tells how and where to find treasure in the waters of England and the Balearic Islands.

Sunken Treasure: How to Find It
One of the world's foremost underwater salvors shares a lifetime's experience in locating and recovering treasure from deep beneath the sea.

True Treasure Tales – Gar Starrett Adventures
The Secret of John Murrell's Vault
The Missing Nez Perce Gold

Let's Talk
Treasure Hunting

By
Charles
Garrett

ISBN 0-915920-91-6
Library of Congress Catalog Card No. 92-62659
Let's Talk Treasure Hunting
Copyright 1992
Charles Garrett

First Printing, December 1992
Second Printing, January 1994

Book and cover design by Mel Climer

For FREE listing of treasure hunting books write

Ram Publishing Company

P.O. Box 38649   •   Dallas, TX 75238

Let's Talk Treasure Hunting...

Contents

By Charles Garrett

Treasure Hunting Texts
Treasure Recovery from Sand and Sea
The New Successful Coin Hunting
The New Modern Metal Detectors
Treasure Hunting Pays Off
Treasure Hunting Secrets
With Roy Lagal
Modern Treasure Hunting
Modern Electronic Prospecting

True Treasure Tales
The Secret of John Murrell's Vault
The Missing Nez Perce Gold

Charles Garrett

About the Author

The name of Charles Garrett ranks high on any list of those men and women who have pioneered the development and use of metal detectors...whether for discovery of treasure...for security...or, for any other reason. The Garrett name is even more directly associated with the term "modern metal detectors" and the use of computerized microprocessor controls on a detector. His company was granted the first U.S. patent for use of a computer chip in a detector and his Grand Master Hunter CX (Computer Express) and Ultra GTA (Graphic Target Analyzer™) detectors have blazed an amazing trail which all other detector manufacturers are now seeking to follow. It is appropriate that he title this new book *Let's Talk Treasure Hunting* since his newest instrument, the Grand Master Hunter CX III, is the first detector that actually *talks* to help find treasure.

Charles Garrett did not set out to become a leading manufacturer of metal detection equipment. He prepared himself well, however, to become one of the world's foremost treasure hunters. Since boyhood he has been enthralled with stories of hidden wealth...tales which brought excitement to his semi-rural youth in the Piney Woods of Deep East Texas. Throughout his life he has continually sought to learn all that he could about techniques and equipment for treasure hunting.

Young Charles' initial interest in outdoor adventure occurred at about the age of 12 when he discovered his first "cache"...old *National Geographic* magazines in the attic of his aunt's home. Stories such as the amazing discovery of King Tut's tomb kindled a fire that burns to this day. The young man made a wish that someday he might experience his own adventures in God's great outdoors and then write about them.

After graduation from Lufkin High School and service in the U.S. Navy during the Korean conflict, he earned a degree in electrical engineering from Lamar University in Beaumont and began his business career in Dallas with Texas Instruments and Teledyne Geotech.

Some three decades ago, then, Mr. Garrett was a young electrical engineer deeply engrossed in development of systems and equipment required by America's fledgling space effort. In devoting himself to his lifetime hobby of treasure hunting, however, he also designed and built metal detectors in his spare time. Because his detectors were obviously more effective than any available commercially, they became popular with fellow treasure hunters for whom he was soon making them. This avocation became a career when he founded Garrett Electronics to produce his inventions.

Today, the name Garrett stands as a synonym for the treasure hunting metal detector. Mr. Garrett himself is known as the *Grand Master Hunter,* also the name of his company's first computerized instrument, described at the time as "the finest metal detector ever manufactured."

Along the way, Mr. Garrett has become recognized as an unofficial spokesman for the hobby of treasure hunting and the metal detecting industry through a long list of honors, personal appearances and books. He is the author of several major works which have been accepted as veritable "texts" for treasure hunting.

Mr. Garrett's metal detector expertise has also carried him into the allied fields of security screening and crime scene investigation. While learning how metal detectors could be of value in law enforcement and security, he has participated in and sponsored numerous seminars and worked with law enforcement and other governmental bodies in an effort to help them develop new metal detectors as a tool for security and crime scene management. Garrett is now the foremost manufacturer of security metal detection equipment in the world. Not only do its famed Magnascanner and Super Scanner instruments protect air travelers all over the world, but they have been honored as the choice to safeguard historical and cultural treasures, Olympic athletes, presidents and kings.

He is married to the former Eleanor Smith of Pennington, TX, who has played a key role in the growth of Garrett Electronics. They have two sons and a daughter.

As a graduate engineer and a businessman, Mr. Garrett introduced discipline to the manufacture of metal detectors. He has generally raised the standards of metal detecting everywhere, while the hobby has grown from a haphazard pastime to almost a science.

Garrett quality is known throughout the world. From the beginning, Charles Garrett vowed "to practice what I preach" — in other words, to test his equipment in the field...to insure it will *work* for customers regardless of ground conditions and environment. Thus, with a metal detector of his own design he has searched for and found treasure on every continent except Antarctica. He has also scanned under lakes, seas and oceans of the world.

Hal Dawson
Editor, Ram Publishing

Dallas, Texas
Winter 1993

By Charles Garrett

Author's Note

This book will teach you how to find treasure! Not treasure buried far away...in another city...another state...another land, but treasure buried literally in your own back yard.

The mistake too many individuals make when they set out to hunt is ignoring nearby treasures while they speed off in search of Captain Kidd's buried chest or that fabled Wells Fargo box hidden by Butch and Sundance.

Successful treasure hunters have learned that there are dozens of "little treasures" concealed in practically every yard or park of any city or town — valuables that were lost just this morning or long ago...yet, all lost and forgotten, but nevertheless well worth finding. It may be more than just a little treasure. It may be a hermit's cache of gold coins...a farmer's "post-hole bank," his wife's "butter-and-egg" money buried in the garden. These are the treasures that this book will teach you how to find.

Who can find this lost wealth? Practically anyone...young or old, male or female, retired person searching almost full time or the weekend vacationer. Success will come in direct proportion to effort expended...and, sometimes the effort will be just walking down a beautiful and sunny beach.

You can spend but a few minutes a day in searching or do it for a lifetime. Coins in a park, jewelry on the beach, gold nuggets in a mountain stream or a buried money cache. Any of these may be *your* treasure, and this book will tell you exactly how to find it.

In *Let's Talk Treasure Hunting* we'll do just that...talk treasure hunting! This is not a metal detector instruction manual. Writing that is a chore for a detector manufacturer. Instead, this book contains instructions that will take you to the very heart of treasure hunting...the research and field searching that result in the excitement of finding instant wealth buried at your very feet.

Man and boy, I've spent more than five decades hunting treasure, and some have said that I'm good at it. I'll offer no opinion except to say that I believe I've found more than my share. And, as you can see from the above timetable, I've found it with and without metal detectors.

Basically, however, my life has been spent developing search and recovery skills that others did not know or were not willing to take the necessary time to learn. And, that's what this book is about...sharing my skills and techniques to help you perfect your abilities while you pursue the fascinating hobby of treasure hunting...a hobby that can not only pay for itself but can prove *very* rewarding.

Whether your goal is a "grand treasure," one you must spend considerable time researching and recovering, or whether you just want a new hobby that will let you enjoy yourself while finding pocket change in the park or on a beach, this book will guide you.

Heed this warning before you start: once you discover that first "treasure" — be it a one-cent coin, valuable ring or gold nugget — you'll risk becoming hooked on treasure hunting for life.

And, you'll love it!

Charles Garrett

Garland, Texas
Winter 1993

Introduction

The appeal of treasure hunting is universal. It transcends all boundaries of age, sex, personality and social status. The desire to seek and find hidden wealth is as old as mankind.

This book then is all about treasure hunting (THing), with specific instructions on the use of modern metal detectors. Many of THing's techniques are exactly the same, whether you decide to use a detector or rely solely on your instinct and eyesight. Either way, this is the book for you! Read on while *we talk treasure hunting*!

Now, THing is difficult to define because it can mean so many different things. Basically, it is the search for and recovery of anything that *you* consider valuable. That's right, only you can determine what's treasure and what's not. Coins, costume jewelry, money caches and relics are all treasure just the same as gold and jewels or whatever else you are looking for.

No matter what the target, THing is an absolutely universal outdoor hobby! Anyone can hunt treasure with equal intensity anywhere on the face of the earth or under its waters. Each individual decides how much energy is required for participation in the hobby, and the decision can be changed from day to day or even from one minute to the next. The hobbyist can hunt for hours a day or for just a short while; the hunting may be strenuous or involve little exertion.

Treasure hunting sites are equally optional. While hidden wealth can be sought at exotic foreign locations, many successful THers swear that the ideal hunting ground is one's own back yard or neighborhood.

Treasure hunting with a metal detector simply adds a modern wrinkle to an accepted ancient pastime. Some people want (or, expect) to strike it rich the very first time they turn on a detector, while others are content to find little more than a few coins in the local park. Some individuals hunt with a detector for the excitement of digging a treasure out of the ground, while others are fascinated by the "historical" discoveries they make. Some find joy in returning lost class rings and other valuables to their rightful owners. Others enjoy displaying in their homes the treasures they have discovered. There are some who write magazine articles and share their treasure hunting techniques with others. Yet, some simply appreciate another opportunity for getting out into God's great outdoors. Any treasure they find is icing on the cake.

Treasure hunting is an ideal hobby for any young person. It channels natural energy and curiosity, while providing opportunities for essentially harmless adventure and excitement. The hobby is perhaps even more suitable for mature men and women — yes, senior citizens — whose health permits (or requires) light outdoor exercise. Equally as important to the older generation can be the aura of adventure this hobby will bring to otherwise placid lives. Treasure hunting generates an opportunity for excitement and suspense without requiring the rigors or expense of lengthy travel and elaborate equipment.

Truly, seeking lost treasure fascinates everyone. And, it is a hobby that can literally pay for itself since it offers financial rewards as well as the benefits of healthy exercise and outdoor activity. Finally, no matter what a person's age, health, financial status or social standing...nothing can compare with the sheer thrill of discovery — whether it be that first coin...a ring...a gold nugget...an outlaw cache. The joy and excitement enrich both the spirit and the pocketbook.

This *Treasure Hunting Text* provides basic information on THing — the research required to select targets as well as the techniques for recovering them. Moreover, it will explain the operation of appropriate modern THing detectors. Simple discussions and outlines of scientific principles that govern the process of metal detection will be given as illustrations.

General Treasure Hunting

What we mean by "general" treasure hunting is just simply searching for *all* types of treasure — coins, relics, money caches, artifacts and other objects that usually have monetary or historical value.

General treasure hunting techniques involve the study of all applications as presented in this book. We realize that approximately 95% of the people who use metal detectors search for coins and that probably more than two-thirds of these hobbyists search *only* for coins. There is always the opportunity, however, for even a dedicated coin hunter to encounter a good lead that requires expertise unrelated to that aspect of metal detection.

If you're interested in THing, you're probably an inquisitive person by nature. You want to find out what's just over the horizon...around the next bend...or, under the next layer of soil. If so, great success in any field of THing can be yours... especially if you use a quality metal detector. All you need now is knowledge.

First, learn all there is to know about your metal detector — its searchcoils, accessories, modes of operation and capabilities. Put your study into action with practice, especially in the field. Dedicated and persistent field training will prepare you to meet successfully all treasure hunting situations that might arise.

For instance, you may be searching in a field and stumble over the foundation of an old building. It could pay you here to search this area especially carefully, using techniques specifically required for detecting money caches. If you're using a detector, you may need to switch to a larger searchcoil and scan around this foundation thoroughly.

Treasure hunting has become a family hobby...husband, wife and children all become dedicated treasure hunters. Sometimes only the man of the household enjoys the hobby, but I know of some wives who will go hunting alone when the husband can't go. Often, children become more proficient than their parents. Hunters, fishermen, campers, vacationers and backpackers are adding metal detectors to their sports gear.

Treasure hunting is healthful!

Who can deny that outdoor activities are healthful? Treasure hunting certainly takes you out of doors into the fresh air and sunshine. Scanning a detector over the ground all day, stooping to dig hundreds of targets, hiking several miles over the desert, or climbing a mountain to reach a ghost town...all of this can stimulate the heart and lungs while putting new demands on unused muscles. But, this is where an extra side benefit is realized. A "built-in" body building program is a valuable *plus* of treasure hunting. Leg muscles firm up, flab around the middle begins to diminish as excess pounds drop off, breathing improves and nights of restful sleep foretell a longer, healthier life.

Treasure hunting is profitable!

It is also simple and easy. Why not begin by considering the hobby of coin hunting? The majority of all treasure hunters begin their new hobby by hunting for coins. Countless millions of coins have been lost and await recovery by the metal detector hobbyist. More coins are being lost every day than are being found...and this has been going on for centuries!

Many persons who begin by scanning with their detectors only for coins often extend their hobby into other areas of treasure hunting. Searching ghost towns and old houses for hidden money caches, and hunting in trash dumps for relics and rare bottles can be very rewarding. One treasure hunter

Treasure hunting is a family hobby that attracts men, women and children of all ages with energy, curiosity and a love for harmless excitement and adventure.

found $41,000 in currency in a metal box that was cached in an old dumping ground. Another man in Idaho found a $20 gold piece estimated to be worth hundreds of thousands of dollars. Countless small fruit jar and "post hole" money caches are uncovered each year.

Most important to many people is the awareness and enjoyment of treasures of nature that God has placed upon the earth for all of us to find. Whether the "big money treasure" can be found is never the point. It is truly gratifying to see nature in its purest form all around and to be a vital part of it. This alone could well be the greatest treasure.

Educational factors related to treasure hunting can be equally stimulating. Relics and artifacts of bygone eras raise many questions. What happened to the people who lived and prospered where only faint traces remain to mark the existence of a once-thriving city or town? Why was the area left deserted? These and other mysteries can usually be solved with proper research and examination of the artifacts found.

Research

Many find it amazing that the successful treasure hunter appears to remain fresh and eager, while the mediocre THer runs about constantly in a helter-skelter fashion, chasing some sort of will-o-the-wisp...never being really satisfied or successful.

To succeed you must hunt correctly and in the right places. Of course, a lot of treasure is found by accident, and all of us dream of finding that "big one" simply by stumbling over it, but that is hardly the way to go about intelligent THing. Most good discoveries result from research.

Hidden wealth can be sought — and found — anywhere...at an exotic location such as this old mountain cabin or right in one's own neighborhood.

Whether you use a detector or not...whether you hunt in the park or on the beach...whether you are a coin hunter, cache or relic hunter, or a prospector, research is vitally important. It is a basic tool you cannot neglect to use if you want to enjoy success.

Research is a key to successful treasure hunting.

In fact, without proper and adequate research, you are shooting in the dark. Your efficiency and likelihood of successful recovery increase proportionately as the amount of your research increases. Without research you may not be as successful as you should or could be since 95% of a successful recovery usually depends on research. Even the world's finest metal detector can only inform you about what is beneath its searchcoil.

It is sad, but true, that most THers do not educate themselves on the correct usage of research. They do not go to the trouble to acquire correct data on treasure sites. They just don't hunt where the treasure is located.

As you might expect, when people such as this use a metal detector, they usually don't learn enough about that instrument either. Yet, they are the first to give up, perhaps blaming the detector for their failure.

Always remember that you must go where the treasure is located. You won't find treasure where it is not; you will find treasure where it is! Most of the time, in order to find where a treasure is located, you must carry out a certain amount of research. You must study, read, and follow up leads. It's wise to talk to people. In short, do your research.

Many Prospects

For the THer who takes pride in his or her efforts, however, the greatest difficulty is deciding which of the dozens or hundreds of leads to follow. People such as this try to avoid "bum steers." They use their brains and they *think*. Common sense is a big factor in successful treasure hunting. Dedicated THers don't search for one treasure. They keep many leads on the back burner and are always looking for new leads to follow. Often in researching one story, you will run across information that applies to another. The THer who is *serious* about this will select several treasure leads to follow and collect all possible information on every one of them. Then each lead can be followed as far as possible, and the THer may even let it lie dormant for a while...allowing the subconscious work on it while waiting for new leads to develop. This type of serious THer may make only one major find a year, but often that is more than enough to repay the effort.

Many "in-depth" books have been written on the subjects of THing and THing with a metal detector. Many of them have been published by Ram Publishing Company. Some of these books should be on your bookshelf and should be read often. Use the order blank at the back of this book.

Living the Hobby

The successful THer lives and breathes the hobby. It is always on his or her mind. Consequently, everything that person reads and everyone they talk with are potential sources of the fresh treasure leads and data they need to help in their work.

If you are a coin hunter, for instance, you can find current coins all day long at the park, playground and along grassy strips near parking meters. If you really want to start finding old and rare, valuable coins, however, you must do your research. You must learn where the old settlers' campgrounds, carnival and fairground sites are located. These are the valuable hot spots; here you will find treasure that makes hunting profitable. This same principle applies to any other kind of THing. If you are looking for gold, you have to search where precious metal has already been found. Gold and silver have been mined in tens of thousands of locations throughout the world, and to have the greatest chances of success, you must determine which of these are the best places to prospect. Relic and cache hunters must also do their research. Find the hot spots, then put your expert detector knowledge to work. It will pay off!

If you have been hunting treasure for almost any length of time, you have probably run across mention of the word *patience.* Absolutely and positively...unless you possess a great amount of patience and put it into practice, you won't be as successful as you could be.

Experienced cache hunters have learned that success comes as infrequently as once in a dozen tries. Consequently, a person without patience to spare will surely give up long before success rolls around.

As you might imagine my work over the years has allowed me to develop friendships with a great many men and women who have achieved outstanding success as THers. Without exception these people possesses an overabundance of patience. They know that you don't find treasure every time you look for it or whenever you switch on a detector. They know and have preached on many occasions that patience must be in your tool kit if you are to be successful.

Hard Work

Successful treasure hunting must be considered work. In fact, it can be one of the hardest jobs a person can undertake. You could sit on a rock all day long with patience to spare, but you would accomplish nothing more than keeping the rock warm, for that rock will never hatch. To find treasure you must prepare yourself with the right attitude which requires proper research and then getting into the field. There you must hunt with all your might, swinging your detector from dawn to dusk and digging every signal, regardless of how weak or how strong.

Many people enjoy going to a park and scanning a searchcoil back and forth over the ground for a while with discrimination set to its maximum. Occasionally they will dig a coin or two. And, there's nothing wrong with that...if it's what a person wants. Yet, there is a far greater reward in hard work, perspiration and the sound of money jingling in the pocket.

If you're willing to study...

If you're not afraid of hard work...

And, if you're even willing to sweat a little...

Success in hunting for treasure will be yours!

Treasure Hunters

L et's look at the hobby of treasure hunting today to try to learn just what it's all about and just what constitutes a treasure hunter.

Treasure hunting is, indeed, a perfect hobby for all ages! Young and old, men and women, the robust and the handicapped...all can find treasure whether they are using metal detectors or not. Of course, I like to believe that using a properly equipped detector gives one THer the advantage over another who is not so equipped!

As you become more active in the search for treasure you will encounter fellow hobbyists ranging from youngsters just three or four to senior citizens more than 80 years young. There is no age limit! THing is popular because it is fun and rewarding. Even though detectors have been around for many years now, only during the past decade or so has THing really found its place in the outdoor hobby world. As its popularity has grown, so has the broad range of people who enjoy it.

THing can serve as the perfect hobby to involve the entire family. Each member can participate. Even with only one detector all can combine their talents...provided no one individual is assigned all the digging tasks! Of course, it's far better when more than one detector is available, so that everyone can experience the thrill of initial discovery.

Over the years I've seen all of this happen. I've seen wives become as avid THers as husbands, and I've enjoyed watching children begin to join in. In fact, I've known some families in which the children were more successful hunters than their parents. Perhaps it's their sharp ears, or maybe they just have more persistence and the other traits of a THer.

Why They Hunt

Searching for treasure with a metal detector is relaxing, both mentally and physically, in addition to rewarding an individual in so many other ways. Primarily, people hunt treasure for the simple fun of the hobby...for the relaxation and good exercise they get. It gives them something interesting to do and brings a little mystery into their everyday existences. Yes, *mystery*! The THer never knows what will be found until a target is uncovered!

More and more campers, hunters, fishermen, vacationers and backpackers are adding a metal detector to their normal sports gear. They have chosen to let THing with metal detectors fill gaps in their regular outdoor activities, providing added enjoyment for them as well as for other members of their families.

Sure, dad is an avid fisherman. He can't get enough of casting or just watching a cork bob around. When mother and the children get restive, they can turn on their metal detector(s) and "fish" for their own targets. When the "real" fish aren't biting, dad will often want to join them. It's amazing what there is to be found with a metal detector at a popular old fishing hole!

It's Profitable!

Of course, there is an immediate financial reward with each coin found. And, THing will ultimately prove to be *profitable* for any persistent hobbyist. He or she will be surprised how soon they find treasure with enough value to pay for their metal detector. For this reason searching for coins is by far the most popular aspect of the overall hobby of treasure hunting. Of course, it is also popular because coins can be sought — and found — almost anywhere. Expensive and time-consuming trips to ghost towns, prospecting country or oceanside beaches are not necessary. The nearby neighborhood park or schoolyard — within walking distance — can provide both adventure and rewards.

Individuals who have no interest at all in seeking large hidden treasures become dedicated to coin hunting. Many of these individuals, however, gradually extend their new hobby into other areas of treasure hunting. They become relic and cache hunters; they seek nuggets as electronic prospectors; they find themselves to be proficient beach hunters simply by taking their detector along on the family's seaside vacation.

Over the years, we have watched with pleasure as the "old pro" treasure hunter of yesterday has been steadily replaced by the everyday hobbyist. Why has this happened? Because hunting with a metal detector is one of the most fascinating and interesting pastimes ever to capture the imagination of the world...no matter what targets are sought or found!

It's Healthy!

Many people enjoy coin hunting because it is an easy and perfect way to achieve and maintain physical fitness. One of the most valuable fringe benefits of the metal detecting hobby pertains to health. Regular use of a metal detector insures a continual body- building program.

The individual who is not in good physical condition at the outset of the hobby soon feels leg muscles building up and sees flab around the waist diminishing as the spare tire is deflated. Breathing improves, and the heart beats more steadily. And, after a vigorous day of searching in the field, is it any wonder that hobbyists sleep better than their friends who sit and watch?

THing can be excellent therapy for many who are recovering from an operation, illness or injury. Certainly the level of activity must be governed by a patient's physical condition, but this hobby can take convalescents out of doors into fresh air and sunshine. Listening to the hum of a metal detector will also permit their minds to soar far above morbid thoughts of the sickroom. Who can worry about illness or injury when discovering a valuable old coin or pondering the whereabouts of a cache?

We know of many cases of individuals who have rapidly recuperated from long illnesses and operations when they earnestly began the hobby of THing. Even those with heart problems...especially those who require exercise with some constraint...find THing just the ticket for the exact kind of workout they need. This subject of health is discussed in much greater length in Chapter 20.

There are no finer people than today's treasure hunters! I have come to know literally thousands of these wonderful people, and I am convinced they are among the best. They possess all of the worthwhile traits I outline in this chapter, but most important of all they are hard-working people who enjoy the rewards of their own labors. They appreciate nature and the out-of-doors and truly understand the meaning of a good day's work and the rewards that it can bring.

To study treasure hunters let's divide them arbitrarily into three categories I'll call amateur, experienced and dedicated.

The Amateur

Most of you will probably fall into the amateur category — at least, at first. And, many of you will never want to leave the amateur category...which is good! Amateurs generally have more fun than the more experienced hunters who are trying to "prove" something or earn a living. An amateur hunts treasure for the sheer enjoyment of doing it. Any objects of value that may be found are but a bonus.

Believe me, however, when I predict that newcomers will uncover more treasure than you can imagine. Too many success stories have occurred in this hobby for me to doubt the ability of any one of you to become proficient.

The amateur treasure hunter decides what treasures he or she wants to find and then goes after them. To be successful in attaining any treasures, however, the novice must make certain of possessing:

    — *Adequate knowledge* and
    — *The right equipment.*

You must gain the knowledge, first, before you can truly know which equipment will be needed. Books such as this are an important first step for the THer in learning about the hobby and the correct equipment with which to pursue it. Let me urge, however, that you try to study books that deal with *modern* equipment and techniques and not learn about the metal detectors and other THing tools of yesteryear. Oh, you'll read some fine and colorful stories in these older guidebooks. Such stories can be lots of fun. But, just remember that modern detectors are many times more capable than those *obsolete* instruments whose praises are being sung so lovingly and delightfully.

Where else can you uncover knowledge about modern metal detectors? A dealer, of course, can be an important source of such information. Treasure hunting clubs will include members with all levels of experience, from novice on up. Most of them are always interested in new equipment. You can learn much from these other THers, plus enjoy the fellowship of our great fraternity. The THing magazines contain interesting stories and will often discuss new detectors. Their ads will prove especially helpful in introducing you to new equipment.

Once you know what sort of treasure you want to look for and how you want to go after it, you'll be able to select the *right* equipment. Please let me emphasize the importance of using the right kind of metal detector wherever and whatever you decide to hunt with one. I urge your close attention to Chapters 3 and 6 which discuss the various types of THing and the proper detector to techniques that will be required.

Experienced and Dedicated

We listed three kinds of treasure hunters, but I've spent a great deal of time on the amateur. That's as it should be since less experienced treasure hunters comprise a primary audience for this book. At the same time, I want to introduce new and modern detectors to the more advanced hobbyists and dedicated treasure hunters who have not yet tried them. Or...who still don't believe the claims made for today's new detectors!

Just who are these experienced treasure hunters?

For the most part they are men and women who make their living in a field closely allied to treasure hunting. Two good examples are metal detector dealers themselves and the operators of diving shops. These semi-pros sell equipment to

THers, and they spend their spare time using it themselves. You'd expect people selling such equipment to keep up with the latest developments. For the most part, they do, and they will certainly make this expertise available to customers. How effectively the experienced THer adapts his or her techniques to the use of new instruments with increased capabilities will determine the true level of professionalism that each THer can achieve.

At the top of the heap are the very few who try to make their living by discovering treasure. These are men (and some women) of whom seldom is heard. They are individuals who work quietly and alone, for the most part. They may pursue a treasure literally for years without even picking up a detector. Research is their keyword. They go looking for a specific treasure only when they are relatively certain where it is...and absolutely certain that it exists. Their finds may be few, but they will also be large.

Such veteran treasure hunters need no urging to try out new equipment and new ideas. They understand that someone seeking a large, missing treasure – in competition with others just as experienced and proficient – needs every advantage possible. That new, deeper-seeking, more sensitive detector may be just the instrument that can find the treasure that other detectors have been passing over.

Although I have stated that the amateur or beginning THer presents the primary audience for this new book, I believe that it will be welcomed as well by more experienced THers who want to learn all they can about new detectors and more creative ways of using them. Presenting such information is a goal of *Let's Talk Treasure Hunting*.

Some years ago a leading treasure magazine asked me to summarize the basic attributes of a successful treasure hunter. In studying the answers that I gave at that time to this magazine I can't see any changes that have occurred in the ensuing years. Some of my concepts might have modified somewhat, but my basic description of a successful THer remains about the same.

Just what are these quirks of the successful THer's nature that differentiate him or her from anyone else? Now, it's true that just about anyone who likes the outdoors and possesses even a little curiosity will enjoy "hunting around" for treasure. Some healthy exercise is guaranteed, and financial rewards may be more tangible, depending upon the diligence (and luck) of the hobbyist.

Becoming a successful THer is far more difficult. Expertise with a metal detector is never enough; it takes a "special" kind of person. By studying the following characteristics I hope that you can determine how successful you might become as a THer.

1. Desire to Find Lost Treasure.

This characteristic is basic to any good THer. It demands both the *belief* that lost treasure is waiting to be found and the *curiosity/craving* to want to find it. It is this *desire* that continually brings a coin hunter back to parks and playgrounds time and time again, even while he or she is seeking out new places to hunt. The belief that treasure is waiting to be found draws relic hunters miles off the map into wilderness areas or keeps them seeking out known battle areas for "that" rusty Civil War pistol. It is the firm conviction that nuggets await that drives the amateur prospector with pan and metal detector into the gold fields. *Curiosity* wonders how the nuggets will look on jewelry, while *craving* measures their value in the marketplace.

Common sense dictates that lost coins and jewelry abound on any beach where people play or have played. It is the *desire* to find them that translates this common-sense knowledge into a deep belief that valuable jewelry, coins and the like are simply awaiting discovery. The successful THer continually says to him or herself that if he or she does not find the treasure, it will be found by somebody else. This characteristic, therefore, is a *desire that transcends belief!*

2. Interest in History.

This important characteristic often spells the difference between average, hard working THers and those whose brilliant successes make them outstanding. Historical knowledge leads to grand recoveries, but historical knowledge is not achieved without hard work...work determining facts and dates that can sometimes seem dull and uninteresting.

The successful THer, however, thrills to research that might uncover a cache lost for years or a hidden lode of treasure. They enjoy reading historical books and histories of events at all levels, local as well as national. They seek out abandoned houses, settlers' campgrounds, ghost towns and scenes of battles. They stop to read the historical markers on the highways, the plaques on obscure buildings. They enjoy gossip from the past about "whatever happened to so-and-so" and "where their money went" and such. They welcome stories about loot missing from old crimes. Always, they are seeking the natural disaster, the lost battlefield, the quietly wealthy miser.

Cache hunters especially display this characteristic. They can begin their long journey with but a single fact. Sometimes it is as obvious as, "A wealthy man farmed here and died without any heirs." More often, it is simply, "There was a farmhouse here once." From this single fact — or rumor! — they seek information until such a full scenario is developed that they need only follow it to discover where to dig.

3. Patience.

This simple virtue presents such obvious rewards that it is envied by all. How many have prayed for patience? Then, demanded that it be granted to them "right now!" Patience is so important and vital that it is needed by all — and needed, yes, immediately.

It is a trait that must be included in the make-up of any successful THer, for many disappointments generally precede "striking it rich." Certainly, failure is not *expected*; indeed, each spadeful of earth is lifted or each rock is moved away with the expectation that treasure awaits. The successful THer, however, works to transform any fruitless efforts of today into building blocks or stepping stones that will lead to tomorrow's worthwhile goals.

18

Whenever a novice sets out to hunt for treasure that person must remember that it takes *time* for an individual to become proficient in *any* endeavor.

The successful THer certainly enjoys the fruits of today's recoveries, but also understands that much effort is required to plant seeds of the trees that will eventually bear such fruit.

4. Interest in Analysis.

This trait, too, is related to curiosity...the successful THer must develop the ability to be inquisitive about places and things and to enjoy analyzing data about them. False leads must be discarded even as true leads are pursued. All facts about a potential recovery must be studied and analyzed. Let's say that you have been "assured" that a treasure was buried atop a mountain. How did it get there? Why did someone climb so high to bury it? Why wasn't it hidden at the base of the mountain? Maybe it was. *Find out!*

Discovering treasure need not always be hard. The successful THer who is keenly interested in analysis knows that treasures are simply hidden and await discovery. The best way to locate them is to seek direct answers to simple questions. An understanding of the importance of analysis helps develop these questions.

5. Not Afraid of Hard Work,

This trait naturally sounds negative since nobody *likes* hard work...it's the results of hard work that make it endurable!

The successful THer, however, truly has no fear of it. And, that's what it takes. Money and other valuable prizes don't fall from trees or wash up on the beach. Many hours and days of hunting are usually required before a truly worthwhile treasure can be discovered. Before you stoop to recover *that* target, you will have bent over countless times to dig and inspect nothing but useless trash.

Success rarely comes with ease. For the successful THer, it comes accompanied by what seems like gallons of perspiration pouring off the brow and pound after pound of soil that must be washed from clothes. The successful THer understands that for success to be worthwhile, it must be worth working for.

6. Love of Travel.

Success demands that you always be ready to follow the results of your curiosity, your research, your analysis and your hard work...even if it takes you miles away across county and state lines. Part of the thrill of research and analysis is to uncover clues that point to treasures far away.

The successful THer always displays faith in such efforts by following the clues they unearth...and, following them without procrastination. That's important...being *ready*! How many times have I and other good THers said, "Well, the next time I go to this-or-that-place, I'll look into that good lead." Then, years pass by, and the "next time" eventually finds that a "good lead" turns out to be an impression in the dirt of an iron pot that *someone else* recently pulled from a hole.

Some day I'm going to write a book that includes the story about how the widow of the legendary Pancho Villa asked me to help her recover caches hidden by that Mexican bandit. I promised her I'd help "later on," but in the meantime the lovely lady died.

7. Interest in Other's Work.

The successful THer is genuinely interested in any treasure story — no matter how it turns out. You must be prepared to spend time studying the successes and failures of others. Personal experience is absolutely necessary, but you should also benefit from the wisdom of others that is available through books, videotapes and magazines.

The successful THer has a good reference library and uses it regularly to learn more about all phases of the hobby. Even when you disagree with someone, ideas and opinions of that person can challenge your imagination, and you profit from the opportunity of measuring them against your own beliefs.

Experienced treasure hunting authors have willingly and gladly shared their lifetimes of experience with you. They have been honest because they have no reason to lie. As the great diver (and, my good friend) Bob Marx likes to say when asked why he gives so much advice freely and willingly, *"There's enough treasure for all of us!"*

Benefit from the experiences of Bob and others like him. Perhaps you can even use one of their failures as a stepping stone toward your own success.

8. Interest in Companionship.

Treasure hunting can be a lonely pastime, but a real *loner* isn't going to be successful. You must have help, and you must not be afraid to ask for it. Help in research...help in selecting equipment...help in every phase of your discovery and recovery. Why, the person you ask may have once sought the same answer!

When you deal with equipment dealers, metal detector and otherwise, try to benefit from their knowledge and experience. Listen closely; you may be surprised what you learn if you remember to listen to the message, not the messenger.

Look for the opportunity to join a THing club that will let you pool your knowledge. Certainly, you're not going to give out your good leads, nor can you expect to receive them from others. You can expect, however, to meet people with similar interests...people from whom you can learn...people who will learn from you.

9. Specialization.

The field of THing is a broad one, indeed. And, almost all successful THers are truly generalists. (See #12.) Each of the good ones, however, started out by selecting a specific type of treasure to seek...then, they pursued that type of treasure with absolute determination and diligence.

Do you seek coins? Are you going to track down caches? Will you be looking for relics or gold? Will you hunt on the beach or in ghost towns?

Choose your field of interest; then, study it carefully. Read stories and instruction manuals about that type of hunting. Try to talk to those who have been successful hunting the treasures you plan to seek. Select sites with your specific targets in mind; study equipment designed to seek them out.

10. Interest in Equipment.

The successful THer is keenly interested in all types of THing equipment, especially metal detectors...their capabilities and their possible limitations. One manufacturer may be favored, but the products of all are studied regularly through personal use and study of the trade press...analyzing field test reports and reading advertisements.

A good rule of thumb for any THer, novice or old-timer, in choosing a piece of equipment to buy is, first, to select the best equipment available for the type hunting you have chosen and based on what you can afford. Then purchase a more expensive model of the same equipment. This does not mean that the successful THer always uses the most expensive equipment available. He or she does use, however, a true all-purpose or universal metal detector designed for hunting multiple types of targets. More information on how to buy a detector is included in Chapter 6.

Certainly, if a specific type of target is chosen, such as coins, beach hunting or searching for gold, specialized detectors for those targets are available.

Remember, too, that the successful THer is interested in laboratory and field testing (see below) that a piece of equipment has actually undergone...not its promotional claims alone.

11. Interest in Testing.

The successful THer can't wait to get any new or different piece of equipment out in the field. What do they *claim* it can do? Now, what can I *make* it do? These are the questions that are asked. Answers, supported by extensive field testing, enable THers to understand the limits of their capabilities. The goal then becomes to extend these capabilities...to *squeeze* more from the detector or other piece of equipment than its manufacturer intended. Only extensive testing can make this happen.

Treasure hunters love their hobby because it can lead them to interesting places and be profitable, but most of all they love it because it is fun.

22

Before taking any metal detector into the field, the successful THer first studies all literature supplied with it by the manufacturer. Incidentally, the following *Owner's Manual Test* is one that should be applied to any detector:

What does the *Manual* tell you about a detector? Does it tell you how to use it? Or, does it contain statistics and wiring diagrams? You don't buy a detector so that you can repair it; you buy it to find treasure. Is the *Manual* printed in a format to take into the field or to be stuffed into a desk drawer? In other words, is the *Manual* designed to be used or filed?

Before you buy a detector, ask to see its *Owner's Manual*. You may be surprised.

12. Desire to Hunt All Types of Treasure.

This trait actually supplements #9, above, rather than conflicting with it. After you have become successful in one specific field you will naturally want to expand your expertise into other areas of THing.

What is more likely, however, is that such an event will occur when you lest expect it. You will somehow be exposed to a treasure, a treasure story or a treasure site while you're still learning about your initially chosen targets. Yet, you understand how procrastination can be fatal (see #6, above) to any THer's chance for success. If you've studied the literature of THing properly, you'll know how to go after your new target. And, that's my advice: Go!

Some may call it luck, but success will come to those who are prepared to recognize opportunities and who have trained themselves to follow through to achieve results.

Because there are no age limits to treasure hunting, many so-called senior citizens let the hobby give them fresh air and exercise that they require

During the study of your chosen Thing field, make up your mind that you are going to become the very best. But, always welcome the opportunity to branch out and study other fields of interest. Even though you have decided to become the very best coin hunter, do not hesitate to follow up on leads to a good cache. Know the size searchcoil you will need and be familiar with the thinking of someone who buries a cache.

Don't be afraid of the beach or the gold field. Just make certain that you have the right kind of equipment and know the general principles for using it. Basic theories of metal detector usage apply to all fields. It is in the area of specialization that you will learn little tricks from others and develop those tricks you learn on your own.

Do you recognize yourself in any of the above traits? You probably do or you wouldn't be reading this book. Yet, because many of them are born into certain individuals, you've never before recognized how important they will be in your THing success. Treasure is waiting to be found!

3 – *The Stuff Dreams are Made Of...*

Buried Treasure

Always remember that *treasure* is anything that an individual prizes or considers valuable. This chapter presents an overview of the various types of treasure for which hobbyists usually search, with each type of THing discussed individually in later chapters of this book. Many of these hobbyists use metal detectors, but it is possible to hunt with only your eyes and instinct. Always remember, however, that the individual using a quality, modern detector will have a distinct advantage over a hobbyist who is hunting without one or who is hunting with an old or inadequate instrument. Arm yourself properly and set out for these treasures!

Coin hunting is the searching for and retrieving of lost coins. Countless millions of coins have been lost and await recovery by the THer. Thousands of Indianhead and Wheat pennies, Buffalo nickels, Barber dimes, Liberty and Washington quarters, Liberty Walking half-dollars, silver dollars, early colonial coins, gold coins and many other types are being recovered every day. People are losing more coins today than the coin hunter is finding! Coins are lost everywhere people go, and coins are being found everywhere people have been. Coin hunting is one of the most active family hobbies in America.

The person not familiar with this hobby finds it difficult to believe that coins can be found. "Who loses coins?" they ask. "Surely, there are not enough lost coins to make it worthwhile to buy a metal detector or spend time looking for them!" I have said many times that "any active and experienced coin hunter can find 5,000 coins each year." This is only an average of 100 coins found each weekend for 50 weeks...a reasonable and attainable goal. If you'll apply the principles set forth in my book, *The New Successful Coin Hunting,* you'll easily find 5,000 coins each year and more!

Don't make the mistake of believing there are no coins to be found where you live. If you don't have the experience now, you soon will gain the knowledge to convince yourself that coins are truly found everywhere. The first place every person should start searching is right in his own backyard before branching out from there. Many people erroneously believe there is nothing in their areas worth searching for. The truth is, all the good coin hunting sites will never be cleaned out.

Exploring a ghost town is a popular and rewarding hobby which includes a number of activities. In ghost towns you may discover old coins, perhaps a buried treasure cache, relics or antiques dating back to the earliest settlers, or lost items from only yesterday. Any place people have gathered will produce relics and coins. There are thousands of abandoned town sites, old forts, homesteads and farmhouse locations. The list is endless. Finding a place to search will never be your problem! Finding the time needed to pursue and enjoy your hobby is often more of a challenge. A good metal detector will really help here since most surface items have already been picked up and those remaining will lie below the surface.

Let me tell you about a straw-encased bottle filled with 773 dimes found years ago over the doorway of an old shack near Maitland, FL. All the coins were dated prior to 1918. There were 46 of the rare 1916-D's, worth more than $100 each, two 1895-O's, worth more than $50, and 10 1904-S's, worth more than $10 apiece. The numismatic value of the other coins brought the total value of the cache to over $5,000, with today's valuation many times more than that amount.

The most significant aspect of the find, however, is that when the coins were hidden they were probably worth little more than their face value of $77.30. In other words, they were probably not hidden by a wealthy person but rather, as the shack would indicate, by someone relatively poor. This bears out the old cliche that, "treasure is where you find it."

Cache hunting is seeking money or valuables that have been put away or cached by someone, the little old lady's "hard times" coins she buried in a jar in the garden 50 or 100 years ago, the old man's "bank" jar he kept hidden in the bottom of a fencepost hole or, the washtub filled with gold coins. These are all "caches!" There are many, many thousands of these treasures waiting for the THer who seeks them out. Often buried only a few inches deep or at arm's length below ground surface, they will remain lost forever if not recovered. Treasures can be found anywhere... in an old chicken coop, between the well and a tree, between two trees, in the ground under the horse stall, in the walls of houses and barns, etc.

Collecting and studying *battlefield relics* constitutes an interesting pastime for many people. Of course, the great war in this country was the Civil War, and values placed on artifacts and other items from this time are often astronomical. Simple buttons from Union and Confederate uniforms have been sold at open and private auctions for as much as $1,000. Buckles, a favorite item with most collectors, are highly sought and often demand prices beginning as low as $25 for common buckles in poor condition to more than $2,000 for the more rare or ornate ones. The finding of battlefield relics brings history so close that one can visualize it in the making.

The numerous battle and skirmish sites of the Eastern and Western campaigns and naval operations abound in relics and artifacts valued by war buffs and professional collectors. All types of weapons or instruments of the war are being located by the persistent metal detector operator. One misconception of this aspect of our hobby is that all "known" battle areas are protected by state and federal governments. True, certain areas, rightfully so, are strictly "off limits" to THers and particularly all metal detector operators. Yet, there are far more sites that are available for hunting than are restricted. You must seek them out!

Remember, too, that many 18th century *battlefields* in the U.S. were settlements on the frontier of the young nation. Relics from these confrontations are also highly prized.

There's Treasure on the Beach!

On some beaches there are roped-off areas designed for swimming. Search these places first! Strike up a conversation with the lifeguard or concession stand operators. It may be that the swimming areas of bygone days were located elsewhere on the beach. You would certainly want to search those sites. Also, lifeguards may know where rings and valuables are reported to have been lost. Try working along the water's edge at both low and high tides as both could be profitable. You will encounter much less trash near the water, but remember, some very valuable coins and jewelry have been found back away from the beach in the heavy traffic areas. There are thousands of swimming beaches no longer used. Visit your library and do a little research to locate these resort and health spa swimming areas where much treasure awaits discovery.

My recently revised *Treasure Recovery from Sand and Sea* presents valuable information on beach and underwater hunting for the novice and expert alike.

Searching for gold was the first extensive use of World War II mine detectors acquired as surplus by ex-GIs in the period immediately following World War II. These military veterans had realized the value of their instruments and proceeded to prove it to themselves in the gold fields. Though woefully inadequate by today's standards the awkward metal detectors could 'look behind" the walls of old mines to discover veins that had been overlooked by early-day miners, and they could help locate nuggets.

Today's modern metal detectors can accomplish these tasks − and others in the gold fields − far more competently. Hunting for gold nuggets is a highly popular use of today's metal detectors. The scenery surrounding such searches is usually pleasant and the risk/reward ratio is impressive indeed.

Other than his rock hammer and patience the most important and useful tool of the rockhound who *hunts for rocks, gems and minerals* can be a metal detector. Properly operated, it can prove very rewarding and interesting, but no detector should be used as the ultimate answer to the positive identification of detectable specimens. Detectors should be used as accessories to equipment of rockhounds...accessories which will aid in locating conductive metallic specimens. The human eye cannot see inside an ore specimen to distinguish or identify it, but a good quality modern detector can.

For our purposes, "metal" is defined as any metallic substance of a conductive nature in sufficient quantity to disturb the electromagnetic field of the searchcoil. If your detector responds to a target as "metallic," collect it for future inspection; it contains conductive metal in some form. If the detector responds as "mineral," it means only that the specimen contains more iron mineral than it does metal in a detectable form. In just a few minutes you might find some high-grade metallic sample that has been passed over for years by fellow prospectors or rockhounds.

When searching for high grade specimens of metallic ore, pay close attention to old mine tailings. You may find that a "worked out" area isn't so barren after all. Certain gems, such as the thunder-egg, have a covering of outside magnetic iron. Some forms of jade and even garnet respond to a good detector.

NOTE: Ore sampling can be accomplished only with a detector that is designed for prospecting and is correctly calibrated to give exacting ore sample identification. To learn about, select and correctly use calibrated instruments, read the Roy Lagal's new book, *Gold Panning is Easy,* or the book that he and I wrote, *Modern Electronic Prospecting,* both from Ram Publishing Company.

Research

Where do successful treasure hunters *find* all those wonderful prizes? That's easy! They find them anywhere people have been — which is practically everywhere. Once a person has begun the fascinating hobby of THing he will no longer need to be convinced that treasure just waits to be found. He will soon have the problem that other hobbyists face — simply too many places to search. When you begin finding treasure, you will discover that the number of places to search is truly endless.

Treasure is where you find it. You may diligently seek it or you may stumble upon it. The choice is yours. You can increase your chances of finding treasure one thousandfold if you will learn how to research projects through to successful conclusion. Without research, treasure discovery comes only by chance and luck...and the booty is often of little value.

Treasure found by accident represents but a small percentage of that found by persons using good, acceptable research practices. Research can consume up to 99% of a successful search and recovery undertaking. Without proper research you'll be as lost as a driver without a map in a strange city. You need a waybill...directions to guide you to the best locations. These waybills, these directions, come from many sources, both public and private.

I *never* advise either buying a treasure map or taking the word of anyone else as gospel. You must always find the primary source for yourself. To begin at the beginning involves a study of basic research material and sources. You must know *what* you are looking for and that it exists. Certain forms of treasure hunting require a knowledge about where specific types of treasure, can be found. You don't search for pieces of eight in a city park or seek lost gold rings in a child's sand box. (Even though tiny children's rings and mother's rings are occasionally found there!)

Since failure to prepare groundwork generally results in wasted time, effort and money, I have included this chapter to give you a head start. Also, other chapters contain specific research information.

Unfortunately, there is no one-two-three step procedure I can outline. One hundred people reading this book may begin looking for one hundred different treasures one hundred different ways! The main thing is to *get started* by defining these goals, which you can call...

A Treasure Check List

- ☐ **What are you looking for?**
- ☐ **Does it exist?**
- ☐ **Where is it?**
- ☐ **Will you have clear title to it if you find it?**
- ☐ **Have others looked for it?**
- ☐ **How do you know they didn't find it?**
- ☐ **What will it cost you to find it?**
- ☐ **Is it worth what it will cost you to find it?**

Certainly, these questions are rudimentary, but yet very important. They may appear to apply just to "really big" prizes, but the same questions pertain to coins in the park and all other treasures. What I want to emphasize is that you not go searching for the will-o-the-wisp. Spend your time wisely and efficiently. Don't waste time looking for treasure unless you are sure, based upon your research, it exists. Use the sources listed here and others to discover how to track down the information about the treasure you seek.

Establish your goal. Then believe in this work and your ability to achieve it. Finally, work like the dickens to make it come true.

To repeat a truth, successful treasure hunting can often be 99% research and 1% recovery. Do not think of research as though it were an uninteresting stint in the back room of some dusty, ill-lighted library where you must pore over volumes of scarcely legible books, articles and newspapers. Research can be fun. It can become something you enjoy and look forward to.

When you become obsessed with THing, you'll continually think about it. You'll scan newspapers and magazines for stories and data about local sites. When you talk with people, especially oldtimers, you'll ask them about such-and-such a place. You'll ask them if they remember whether the present park and grandstands are located where they were decades ago. You'll ask them if they remember incidents when individuals lost jewelry and other valuables.

When you read the newspapers, be alert for leads such as news reports of modern day heists and robberies. When a safe, for instance, is stolen, the thieves must do some thing with it. Usually, "hot" items are discarded in some convenient nearby pond or stream. A fellow repairing the roof on one of our Garrett buildings, told me an interesting story. He reported that an acquaintance of his knew of the theft of a private coin collection. Realizing that the property could be traced, the thief hastily threw the collection into a nearby creek. The roofer promised to show me the exact spot. Well, embarrassing as it is "to tell the rest of the story," I delayed too long. A few months later when I tried to locate the roofer, I could not. The fellow had moved and no one knew his whereabouts. So, the moral to that story is, when you hear of a "good one," *Go Immediately.* Don't delay. Check the story to a satisfactory conclusion!

There's an unlimited amount of research information available to you. The only limits will be those you impose upon yourself. Knowing that everyone has shortcomings, you should never rely entirely upon the work of others. When someone is willing to write about a treasure, you can be sure that person has abandoned his search for it for one reason or another. You must analyze the data with a cautious eye. Failure of the writer to complete the research and recovery could be due to lack of funds time, or, simply, interest. But, if a person took time to travel to a site and investigate it, that person must have believed in his story.

Do not become discouraged if in the early stages of your THing activities, you cannot achieve immediate success. Set goals for your success and strive to achieve them. Success will come if you persist.

You must never doubt that you will be successful. Dogged patience, perseverance, continued study and research and field practice are necessary ingredients in the formula of success in this fascinating and rewarding hobby. If you are skeptical and do not continue unswervingly in your quest, you will achieve mediocre results. But, when you one day "round the corner" and begin filling your pouch with coins, jewelry and treasure, then you will know you have "made it" and can look forward to successes of which you may never have dreamed or envisioned.

People write to me telling about new discoveries. I read the newspaper and pick up valuable leads. I see bulletins from treasure hunting clubs and other publications written about THers. Old friends and business associates share their secret places with me. I truly can hardly turn around without locating another new location just waiting to be searched.

Oldtimers can tell you of places you could never learn about from other sources. Use your head; think! For instance, I searched for years before I suddenly realized that coin hunters should be able to find coins under a clothesline. And, sure enough, they were there. You can easily prove to yourself that even the neatest mothers and wives were unable to completely remove all the coins and metal objects from pockets of their children's and husbands' clothes before hanging them out to dry.

Gold Coins Waited

While on vacation with my family I struck up a conversation with a retired postman in a small north central Colorado town. He told me about a long-forgotten city park where a special event had once been held celebrating the founding of the city.

Since gold had been instrumental to the growth of that old mining town, the city fathers decided to bury $5 gold pieces throughout the park for people to find. After a starter's pistol fired, townspeople could race through the park and scratch around looking for the coins. This "treasure hunt" would commemorate the city's founding.

Well, a good time was probably had by all, as they say. But, any detector operator could immediately see the value in searching this area! For decades the gold coins that had gone undiscovered at the celebration just "slept" beneath the surface, waiting for the radio signals of a metal detector. There are many such areas throughout the United States.

Start at Home

Let me emphasize that you should never overlook the possibilities for finding treasure at your very doorstep. Don't make the mistake of believing there is nothing to be found where you live. If you don't have the experience now, you soon will gain enough knowledge to convince yourself that treasures are truly to be found everywhere. The first place every hobbyist should start searching is his own backyard.

I can't tell you how many people have complained to me that there is nothing in their area worth searching for. And, they're talking about an entire town or county! The truth is that it would take an army of thousands of THers, working many years, to search and clean out all the productive areas existing today. And, by that time, think how many more additional items of value would have been lost and would be waiting to be located!

Don't Pity the East!

Over the years I have heard many residents of the East Coast complain that metal detectors are useless in their area because there is nothing there to be found. The first time I heard this I could not understand how anyone could believe it until I began thinking. Yes, detectors were first used in the West where they were utilized primarily for prospecting...looking for nuggets and veins. Most of the instruments manufactured in the early years were produced on the West

Coast. And, discoveries of precious metals are still made primarily in the West, with isolated exceptions.

As a result, residents of the East Coast generally think of metal detectors as being of value only in the search for precious metals; they "logically" conclude that detectors are useless in their particular areas. Of course, this is ridiculous!

The heavily populated East Coast of the United States is one of the world's hottest THing areas. Since this section of the United States was settled first, it stands to reason that more old and, often, more valuable artifacts and coins have been lost there than anywhere else in the country. Since the area still contains the most dense clusters of people, greater numbers of valuable and historic objects being lost there daily.

In searching on the East Coast, the same basic rules given in this book apply. You will search the same kinds of places, using the same techniques for operating your detector. Rewards will be yours. Study your local history; talk to the old-timers; determine where old parks, meeting grounds, towns and communities were located. Where did people once congregate? Here, you will find your personal "hot spots."

About "Hot Spots"

You'll soon discover that so-called "hot spots" for finding coins and jewelry can be found in just about any given area. In other words, people have congregated in some places more than others. It's true today; it's always been so. You can learn about "hot spots" simply by observing people as they go about their daily routines. Drive over to your school or college campus. When you are at church, watch the people coming and going...see where they stand and talk, where their children run and play, where cars let out passengers. Just a little common sense and observation will enable you to increase your finds.

In a children's park or playground some of the better places to search are under swings, slides and gymnastic equipment. Naturally, children who turn head over heels are going to lose things. Coins are commonly lost in picnic areas where people sit or lie down.

Your imagination will be called on when you investigate areas that are no longer used by the public. From your own experiences try to visualize where the crowds would have gathered. Then, develop "crisscross" searching techniques that will let you sample the particular areas you have selected. As you search different areas, keep accurate count of the coins and jewelry you find and where you found them. From this data you will soon learn the probable location of the best places to search. Some hobbyists seem to be able just to walk into an old park and immediately begin looking in the exact spots where valuables are to be found. Experience will enable you to become such a THer!

Use Your Ears

Where were the old schools or meeting places located 50 or 100 years ago? At what locations did people gather in the past as they no longer do today? What about training camps, CCC camps, old reunion grounds, settlers' encampments, old communities that are now ghost towns? And, what about the ghost towns of yesterday that have totally disappeared today? The growing urbanization of America has caused many thriving rural communities to cease to exist completely... literally, to vanish from the face of the earth. Crops in the field grow silently where busy people once congregated, transacted business and *lost valuables*!

In your home town where are the long-forgotten fairgrounds, circus and carnival areas...the tent shows that were so popular in the days before air conditioning? What about the old swimming pools and picnic areas? Where were the old train, interurban and bus depots where so many commuters regularly removed coins and tokens from their pockets? There is no way that any single individual can know of all the rewarding coin hunting areas in a community.

Use your ears! Make it a habit to listen to the old-timers. Talk to family, friends, storekeepers — especially the older, retired people of the community who were postmen, bus drivers, merchants, policemen, firemen and the like. These individuals will have a wealth of information that can help you locate valuable THing areas. And, don't ask them simply where you can find old coins. Just try to start them talking about the past...their activities and pleasures of yesterday.

What about nearby parks? How old are they? Are they in the same place now they were 50, 75 or 100 years ago? Check the official records of your city. Investigate vacant lots. What used to be there? As you drive through rural communities and small towns, stop to talk with the old-time residents. And, listen to them! You'll be amazed at how many are just waiting for an audience. Let them tell you where the general stores, saloons, banks and cafes used to be. Let them tell you of all the things that people used to do. That old-timer won't know it, but he'll be telling you where treasure is waiting.

Personal Examples

Let me give you an idea of what I mean. About one-half mile from the little East Texas community of Pennington is the site of long-gone Steele Academy. This was a training school for boys that operated for many years before closing its doors. This has proved to be a good THing area.

From a museum curator in the historic town of Cripple Creek, CO, I found the location of an old picnic grounds, high above the city on a mountain top. This park and picnic area was once so popular that the local trolley car company built a track all the way to the park and had cars running continuously, especially on weekends. Think how many coins and other relics, 75 and 100 years old, lie here awaiting the avid coin hunter.

In my own area of Dallas I am familiar with parks that have been in use since before the turn of the century. Here, I have

Continuing success enjoyed by the author, left, and his longtime friend Roy Lagal prove the importance of research in locating and recovering treasure.

recovered numerous valuable coins. Surely, you know of similar parks in your areas.

One excellent method for finding the oldest items is to determine geographically where your town or city was located when it was founded. Often, the present center of the town's activity is far removed from the original center of population.

The Bill Wendels of Florida determined the location of the original site of Tampa, FL. Many relics and coins, including Spanish reales, half dimes, large cents and other denominations were found there. The American coins are dated in the 1830s. Even older coins could still be found because the original town of Tampa was erected just outside Fort Brooke's walls in 1823.

Older the Better

There is no doubt that most coin hunters truly enjoy getting out into the parks, playgrounds and other outdoor areas simply to search for lost coins and valuables. And, they delight at every discovery! But, let's face it — the finds that we enjoy *most* are those with the greatest value. This lets us benefit financially from the hobby. Thus, it behooves us to make the most diligent efforts to seek out and locate the THing areas where the greatest number with the most value are to be found. I hope that each of you shares my special joy in finding something old...a remnant of the past. The half cents, large cents, two and three-cent pieces, half dimes, Liberty-seated quarters...and especially *gold coins*. These are often worth many times, often thousands of times, their face value...yet they provide an additional historical and romantic thrill. Such oins are seldom located in parks, around school yards or in areas of relatively recent occupancy. You must look for older

Research led this treasure hunter to the site of an abandoned service station to hunt for relics and old coins as well as other items of interest and value.

habitations and areas of activity to find these older and rarer coins. This is where *research pays off!*

Research Sources

Modern Day Photographs: The undisputed value in photography lies in the fact that photographs will reveal objects and features you normally do not see or when scanning hurriedly. You can do your own photography or obtain photographs from many public and private sources such as U. S. Forest Service field offices.

Old Photographs: They capture forever the activities of man. Sooner or later a photographer is bound to show up at every recreation site. The photographers of yesterday seemed to enjoy photographing citizens of the day in their funny-looking (to us) costumes. Old time photographs offer a world of information and in many cases the exact spot where recreation took place. Unfortunately, most old photographs are not identified. No one took the time to write, on the reverse side, the site location. But a little research can lead to an understanding of the site that will enable you to have it pointed out by an oldtimer.

Oldtimers: The oldtimer is one source of information that you must never pass up. In fact, these storage vaults of treasure locations should be actively sought out and quizzed for every last scrap of information that can guide you to a fruitful location. When talking with oldtimers about old locations, quiz them about jewelry items that they may know of being lost years ago. Oftentimes they'll tell you of valuable rings and other jewelry items that were lost by their companions. If they'll take you to these treasure sites, all the better.

Bulletin Boards: Located in laundromats or stores and other public areas, these boards often contain notices of lost items. It will pay you to check these places frequently. Why not post your own "Have Detector...Will Travel!" notices on these free bulletin boards?

Park Managers or Proprietors: Oftentimes lost items are reported to managers or proprietors in the hopes the lost article will be found. One fellow I struck up a conversation with at an abandoned park described the probable location of a safe that was stolen by two men approximately 15 years earlier. One of the thieves had told him that they stole the safe and hauled it part way across the dam. During their attempt to open the safe they were fearful of being caught by the police so they rolled the safe down the dam's slope into the water. I investigated the area and determined that the dam was soft earth and, in all probability, the safe quickly sank several feet into the earthen dam below water level. I earmarked that one for future investigation.

Libraries: Here's where you can spend lots of time that can pay off. Unless you're familiar with library cataloging, ask the librarian for help. Tell her you're looking for history books, periodicals, maps and other sources that will list early day recreational areas. Take your time and look through every reference you find. Either use the copier to gather the information you need or take along some 3x5 cards and list each site on a card. The more specific you can be with the librarian as to what you're looking for, the more help you will get.

Newspapers: When you have free time, go down to your local newspaper office and ask to browse through their old newspapers or microfilm of past editions. Scan the lost and found column for items lost by persons visiting local recreational areas. Study the travel sections for information about resort and recreational sites. Read articles that describe severe storms, especially tornadoes and hurricanes, in which homes were flooded or destroyed. These areas could be a true treasure vault of many types of lost valuables. Especially be on the lookout for photographs of people enjoying themselves at play in bygone times.

Departments of Parks and Recreation: Write, call or go by and request lists of all recreational facilities where people might have gathered. Ask them to send you all promotional literature describing the type of sites you're searching for. Don't forget aerial photographs, especially the old ones that show the locations of old recreational sites, many of which may be no longer in use.

Old Atlases: Your library or historical society may have old community issues you can review. From these you can learn the location of long-gone communities, railway and stage stations, fords, Indian encampments and the like. Old city maps will show the location of the oldest recreational parks where you can find, perhaps, the oldest coins...where that gold coin might be waiting.

Yearbooks: School and college yearbooks often abound with photographs taken by young, enterprising photographers. These yearbooks can be a valuable source of recreational sites whose locations could keep you busy for years to come.

Historical Books: More and more historical books seem to be appearing about practically every town, city and county in the United States. And, the authors and editors all seem to try to outdo each other. Rare, even valuable, photographs are often included, along with data concerning activities. The early-day recreational sites are true bonanza locations where you'll want to scan for lost treasure of yesteryear.

Maps : Never pass up the opportunity to scan both new and old maps for location of likely areas.

Museums: Don't be content just to browse through your local museum. Tell the curators what you're looking for; they can dig back into dusty files and come up with some true treasure vault locations you might not find down any other avenues. Be sure to browse photograph and old book departments since valuable relics such as these are often donated to museums. Your local museum can be as good as the library in providing good research material. You are more likely to meet resistance when it comes to trying to work with museum curators and other personnel, so a good idea is to develop an historical research *thesis* of the local area. You may get lots more assistance.

Ghost Town Books: Be on the lookout for books written about ghost towns and old sites of your area. Certainly you'll want to locate these long-neglected treasure vaults and clean them out.

Hotel and Motel Lobbies: They'll almost always have a literature rack containing free brochures that describe various vacation and tourist spots.

Historical Societies: If the town or city is large enough, there'll be a "home" where the historical society has its headquarters. Not only will the persons on duty probably be well versed in local sites of interest, there may be a library of invaluable maps and books that contain the locations of more places than you can search in a year.

U.S. Forest Service: The U.S. Forest Service maintains an excellent photo and map library that may contain photos of areas that are of interest to you. Check with your local Forest Service office or write the Chief, Forest Service, U.S.D.A., South Building, 12th and Independence Avenue, S.W., Washington, DC 20013, for information.

Paper and Timber Companies: These companies have millions of acres accessible to vacationers. Contact them to obtain information on swimming and recreational sites.

National Forests: Write to them and request information and locations of recreational areas open to metal detectors.

National Park Service Recreation Areas: For specific information write to the Regional Office, National Park Service, Room 3043, Interior Building, Washington, DC 20240.

National Cartographic Information Center: Available to you are 1.5 million maps and charts, 25 million aerial and space photographs and 1.5 million geodetic control points. Write to the National Cartographic Information Center, U.S. Geological Survey, 507 National Center, Reston, VA 22092.

U.S. Government Printing Office: The U.S. Government Printing Office offers more than 25,000 books and pamphlets through a centralized mail order office and 24 bookstores throughout our nation. To have your name added to this free descriptive booklet distribution list, write the Superintendent of Documents, U.S. Government Printing Office, Attention: Mail List, Washington, DC 20401.

National Weather Service: Climate data and flooding information will be of interest to every beach and surf hunter. For information about general information offered, write to the National Weather Service, National Oceanic and Atmospheric Administration, 8060 13th Street, Department of Commerce, Silver Spring, MD 20910.

Bureau of Outdoor Recreation: For information on outdoor recreation programs, write to the Bureau of Outdoor Recreation, Department of the Interior, Washington, DC 20240.

State Archives: During normal working hours, you can search through historical documents, maps, charts and prints relating to the history of just about any state. Since the archives are funded by tax dollars, you certainly shouldn't overlook this source.

State Tourist Bureau: Write to your bureau and request specific information related to your investigation.

Municipal Government Information Sources: Cities and towns change with time. Study available maps and look for defunct parks and other gathering places.

River Authorities: A good source of information for old boat landings, river ports, forts and long-past ghost towns.

Local Treasure Hunting Clubs: If you are not a member, sign up now! Active members will know where the hot spots are. Don't miss out on the rewards that can come from being an active member of your local and/or state clubs. Join national clubs devoted to helping members find treasure.

More Books: This is one of the best sources for finding recreational areas, old as well as current. Check with your local library and bookstores to learn what has been printed.

And Magazines: Treasure and other magazines can be a source of good information, but be cautious. Articles contained in these publications make interesting reading and many contain factual information. But, use common sense when spending time and/or money seeking out the "hot spots" that authors boast about. If the hunting there is that good, would *you* write an article and tell the world about its location? You know that when you talk about your treasure finds, you probably paint a more glowing picture than actually exists. And, probably, the person listening to your story sees it as even more romantic and rewarding than you intended to describe it. Always, if possible, obtain two or three creditable references about a subject before striking out on the treasure trail.

It's Up to You

There is no way that I can stress strongly enough the importance of all the ideas presented in this and the following chapters. Sure, treasure is just waiting to found nearly everywhere, and I am sure that those of you who persevere will find their goodly share. Still, the maximum monetary value in THing and the greatest personal rewards come from finding the old and valuable items...and, finding them as a result of your own research, investigation and hard work. True, you'll probably never actually grow tired of current coins...no matter how many of them you find in parks and playgrounds. But, you'll get so much more pleasure and vastly larger rewards from recovering old and rare items in places you have discovered through your own desire and careful investigative efforts. You can only grow even more enthusiastic as your rewards increase!

In this chapter I have tried to stir your imagination about the great potential of THing...to help you understand how valuables can be found *everywhere*. I hope that you will understand, however, that some effort is required if you are to receive any benefits from THing...and, that *much effort* will be necessary to achieve the maximum benefits. Research, planning and a great deal of investigative work and thought will be necessary.

A section of my book *The New Successful Coin Hunting* includes as many places as I know of or have been told about where coins have actually been found. I have also included lists of the sorts of people you should seek out and listen to. My book *Treasure Recovery from Sand and Sea* deals similarly with treasures from the beaches and waters of the world.

Throughout this book are scattered bits of information designed to help research...that will aid you in seeking out and locating additional sites for THing. I can't repeat enough the simple truism that your success depends entirely upon your effort. Those items that represent lost wealth are there; it's up to you to find them!

Treasure is WHAT and WHERE you find it!

Metal Detectors

It is not necessary to understand the scientific principles of metal detection to use a detector for treasure hunting. You can find coins, rings, jewelry, gold nuggets, caches or whatever you are searching for without knowing how your detector works. For better comprehension of what your detector is doing, however...to recognize why it just made that *peculiar* sound...to understand why it reacts the way it does to metals and minerals...it is helpful to learn how a metal detector works.

In trying to explain how a metal detector operates I've said many times that there's no "magic" to the way it can so easily locate an earring or coin in the grass, buried deeply in soil or rocks, or in the surf. It's all a matter of electronics. That's what I say.

But, yet...there's a bit of "magic" there, too, for every avid THer. In point of fact, a metal detector might simply be an electronic device that detects the presence of metal, primarily through the transmission and reception of radio wave signals. When you're scanning it across a spot of ground, and it makes a noise that alerts you to the presence of a valuable ring or coin several inches below the surface...don't say it isn't magic!

But, let's consider for a minute just what a metal detector is and how it works. If you've read any of my other books, some of this may already be starting to sound a little familiar. As I've pointed out so often before, however, the physical *laws* and the mythical *lore* of THing and metal detecting never change...just the personalities involved and their experiences.

To start, let's consider what a detector is *not*. It is not an instrument (Geiger counter) that detects energy emissions from radioactive materials. It is not an instrument (magnetometer) that measures the intensity of magnetic fields. It does not "point" to coins, jewelry or any other kind of metal; it does not measure the abundance of metal. A metal detector simply detects the presence of metal and reports this fact.

When a coin or other treasure is made of metal — and, most of them usually are — a metal detector can signal their location a reasonable distance beneath its searchcoil. How all this comes about is a somewhat more complicated story.

Metal is detected essentially by the transmission and reception of radio wave signals. This is true of any device designed for that purpose. What distinguishes quality metal detectors such as those manufactured by Garrett from those of lesser quality are the methods by which signals are transmitted and the sophistication with which target information is received, interpreted and passed along to the hobbyist.

When a detector is turned on, a radio signal is transmitted from the searchcoil of a metal detector, generating an electromagnetic field that flows out into any surrounding medium, whether it be earth, rock, water, wood, air or other material. Electromagnetic field lines penetrate metal whenever it comes within the detection path. The extent of this pattern depends upon the power used to transmit the signal and the resistance of the medium into which the signal is transmitted.

The electromagnetic field generated by the searchcoil's transmission causes *eddy currents* to flow on the surface of metal detected by this field. Generating these currents on the metal causes loss of power in the electromagnetic field and this loss of power can be sensed by the detector's circuitry.

Electromagnetic field lines passing through metal and generating eddy currents further disturb the normal electromagnetic field. Simultaneously, a secondary electromagnetic field is generated by the eddy currents into the surrounding medium.

These currents and the resulting distortion of the electromagnetic field are sensed by a metal detector. A receiver in the searchcoil detects these signals at the same time the loss of generating power is being detected. Circuitry of the metal detector simultaneously interprets all these sensations and generates appropriate signals to the operator. The detection device instantly reports that some sort of metallic object appears to be present.

If you think all this interpreting and generating requires complicated electronic circuitry, you're right...especially for a detector that expects to detect deeply and accurately. That's just one of the reasons for the vast differences in the quality — and prices — of metal detectors. Those instruments with more sophisticated circuitry designed to do a better job of sending out signals and then receiving and interpreting them for you simply cost more to develop and manufacture.

But, they find more treasure. And, they find it deeper!

Electromagnetic signals from the detector's searchcoil cause eddy currents to flow on the surface of any metal object (or mineral) having the ability to conduct electricity. Precious metals such as silver, copper and gold have higher conductivities and, appropriately, more flow of eddy current than iron, foil, tin or other less desirable metals. Since metal detectors can "measure" the amount of power that is used to generate eddy currents, the detector can "tell" which metals are the better conductors.

Quite simply, the quality of signals generated, received and interpreted by the metal detector and the ability of the THer to act upon them determines the difference between "digging junk" and finding treasure.

Oh, that it could be so simple!

Penetration of the electromagnetic field into the "search matrix" (that area over which a metal detector scans) is described as "coupling." Such coupling can be "perfect" into air, fresh water, wood, glass and certain non-mineralized earth.

Unfortunately, life is seldom perfect. The search matrix which a metal detector "illuminates" (through transmission and reception of signals) contains many elements and minerals...some detectable and some not, some desirable and some not. A metal detector's electronic response at any given instant is caused by all conductive metals and minerals and ferrous non-conductive minerals "illuminated" in the search matrix by the electromagnetic field. Detection of minerals is, in most cases, undesirable.

And, wouldn't you know it? Two of the most undesirable are also two of the most common: natural iron (ferrous minerals) found in most of the earth's soil and wetted salt found in much of the earth's soil and water. Not only do these minerals produce detection signals, but they inhibit the ability of instruments to detect metal.

When iron minerals are present within the search matrix, the electromagnetic field is upset and signals are distorted. Iron mineral detection, therefore, has presented a major problem to manufacturers and users of metal detectors. Although detection of such minerals may be desirable when a prospector is seeking ferrous black sand or magnetite that could contain gold or silver, it is a nuisance to the hobbyist who is looking for jewelry, coins or similar treasures.

A primary design criterion of any detector, therefore, must be to filter or eliminate responses from undesirable elements, informing the treasure hunter only of those from desirable objects. This is accomplished in a variety of ways depending upon the type of metal detector.

Such words as ground balancing, ground canceling, discrimination and elimination have been used more or less interchangeably over the years to describe the ability of a detector to seek out only desirable targets while ignoring ground minerals, trash and junk.

It is in this area that many of the significant advances have been – and continue to be – made in the design of metal detectors. Electronic engineers have long known that this task could be accomplished through various methods of circuitry which properly manage the normal electrical phase relationship among resistive, inductive and conductive voltage.

Don't let that preceding sentence confuse you. Simple phase shifting itself is a phenomenon basic to the understanding of electricity. Anyone who has studied physics or is familiar with electricity knows that.

It's the *management* of phase shifting that makes detectors so different from each other. Management of this phase shifting to enable a specific metal detector to "dial out" iron mineralization or other undesirable targets, while still permitting the discovery of coins and jewelry, involves highly proprietary knowledge and circuitry protected by U.S. patents. The author and other Garrett engineers, incidentally, hold a number of these patents, including some that are primary in the manufacture of metal detectors.

When you begin studying mineralization, target identification, field applications and other subjects, you will be rewarded by your study of this background material. You will understand what your detector is telling you...why you hear certain signals. You will become better able to determine if the object you have detected is one that you want to dig. Proper and highly efficient operation of a metal detector is not difficult. It does, however, require a certain amount of study, thought and field application.

Depth of Detection

The electromagnetic field transmitted by any detector flows into the search matrix, generating eddy currents on the surface of conductive substances. Detectable targets that sufficiently disturb the field are detected. But, why, you may ask, do some detectors detect *deeper* than others? And, for goodness sakes, why do some detectors even detect *better targets* than others?

The answer is simple. Better detectors detect deeper and they will reject unacceptable targets. Circuitry of these *better* detectors is more intricate, enabling them to penetrate deeper into the soil by avoiding unwanted targets. Not only will this circuitry project a stronger electromagnetic field, it is designed to interpret disturbances in this field with more precision. Of course, the resistance of materials present in the search matrix further determine how deep the electromagnetic field will penetrate.

Of the factors that determine how deeply a target can be detected only the electromagnetic field and the circuitry to interpret its disturbances are a function of the detector itself. Two other important factors, size and surface area, are determined by the individual targets.

Simply stated, the larger a metal target...the better and more deeply it can be detected. Larger detection signals come from targets that produce more eddy currents. An object with double the surface area of another will produce detection signals twice as strong as those of the smaller object, but it will not necessarily be detected twice as far. It is true, however, that a large target will produce the same detection signal as a small target positioned closer to the searchcoil.

Surface Area

Generally speaking, modern metal detectors are surface area detectors. They are not metallic volume (mass) detectors. How a detector "sees" a target will be determined to a large extent by the surface area of a metal target that is "looking at" the bottom of the searchcoil. You can prove for yourself that the actual volume or mass of a target has very little to do with most forms of detection.

With your detector operating move a large coin toward the searchcoil with the face of the coin "looking at" the bottom of the searchcoil. Note the distance at which the coin is detected. Now, move the coin back and rotate it so that the narrow edge "looks at" the searchcoil's bottom. Bring the coin in, and you will notice that it must come closer to the searchcoil to be detected. The mass of metal itself did not change, only the surface area of the coin facing the searchcoil.

Another proof is to measure the distance a single coin can be detected. Then, stack several coins on the back side of the test coin and check to see how far this stack of coins can be detected. You'll find that the stack can be detected at only a slightly greater distance, illustrating that the greater volume of metal has very little effect on detection distance.

Fringe-area detection is a characteristic whose understanding will enable you to detect metal targets to the maximum depth capability of any instrument. The normal detection pattern for a coin may extend, say, nine inches below the searchcoil; the detection pattern for a small jar of coins may extend, perhaps 18 inches. Within these areas of detection an unmistakable detector signal is produced.

Does detection take place outside the detection pattern? You bet! Signals from this detection, however, are too weak to be heard by the operator except in the fringe area directly adjacent to the outer edges of the normal detection pattern.

The ability to hear fringe-area signals results in greatly improved metal detection efficiency and success. If you want to hear such signals, a good set of headphones is a must, along with training in the art of discerning those faint whispers of sound that can signal the presence of a coin in your fringe area. You can develop the ability to hear these signals with practice, training, concentration and faith in your detector and its ability. Those of you who develop fringe area detection capability will discover treasures that other hobbyists miss. Combine your newfound capability with a modern instrument that can detect deeper and more precisely, and you have a treasure hunting team that can't be beat!

How Detectors "Report"

When a treasure hunter is scanning his searchcoil over the ground or in the water, a detector reports information on targets in three ways:

• Increases or decreases in audible volume (universal on all detectors);

• Graphic information presented on LCD meters (sometimes reported in a numerical "code").

• Meter deflections (types of meters can vary greatly, along with the amount and accuracy of the information they present);

Acceptable objects cause the audio or visual indicators to increase in amplitude; unacceptable objects cause the indicators to decrease. Metered target identification indicators can provide additional information concerning the possible "value" of targets.

Learn to listen closely to your detector's signals, and interpret what is "telling" you through sound and meter/LCD indicators. This chapter is essentially continued in Chapter 7 which tells how to search with a metal detector.

Those with a keener interest in metal detectors — especially the new, computerized instruments — should read the final chapter of this book, which discusses the new and different kinds of detectors in greater detail.

Author demonstrates miniaturization with small printed circuit board from modern detector that contains all elements of two boards lying before him.

Selecting a Detector

F or some of you this may be the book's most significant chapter! Selecting the *right* metal detector will be one of the most important steps you take in your pursuit of the hobby of treasure hunting.

Metal detectors are actually easy to evaluate. This chapter should make this task easier for you. Yet, selecting a detector is far more involved than just finding one with all the features you want that costs the "right amount." *Quality* must be your goal. And, if you are diligent, you can recognize it. Quality is never an accident!

Learning more about detectors will enable you to recognize quality more easily. Carefully study the advertising and sales literature of leading manufacturers. Pay attention to facts and look for specifics. Always beware those instruments whose abilities are described only as "hunts deeper" or "more sensitive." Make a chart listing the various brands and types of detectors, their capabilities, and the major features for which advertising claims are made. On the chart note what you like, and don't like, about each of them...also, their cost.

If a manufacturer says a detector will do a particular job, study its literature to determine if in-depth information is

This searchcoil is a product of the computer engineering, design and construction that is necessary in the manufacture of modern metal detectors.

provided to prove that detector's capabilities. Or, have flat competitive statements simply been made about a detector with no proof whatsoever? Visit or contact detector dealers. Talk to them about the various kinds of detectors.

Which instruments do experienced treasure hunters use? Read the various magazines and books published on the hobby. Notice which detectors are being used.

Testing the Instrument

Then, get your hands on one! Turn the detector on. Is it ready to hunt immediately? Modern detectors are. I know that my long-time goal for Garrett detectors has been to enable them to find treasure upon the touch of a single control. Many of my detectors can now do this.

If the detector you are testing is more complicated, first set its audio level. If you are not able to do this, ask the dealer for assistance. See how easily he sets the detector. Does he seem to know what he is doing? If he cannot set the instrument and show you easy steps to operating it, perhaps you should doubt his ability to advise you properly.

Select a detector built by a progressive company that has a continuing program of detector improvement. Does the manufacturer test his own instruments? Does he get out into the field and use them under all kinds of situations? Does he travel to various locations to test varying soil conditions to insure his detectors work regardless of conditions? Are company engineers active in the field?

Pay no attention to magical, fanciful and mysterious descriptions. A detector may be called a "super-duper triple snooper" or touted for its "unparalleled performance" or described as "rarin' to go" with amazing performance. You may be told that "this detector has a trash rejection circuit that is factory-computerized."

Don't fall for the gimmick that "this detector has transistors in it that are the equivalent of a microprocessor" or has "x-many more transistors" than any competitive instrument. Someone may be trying to dump an engineering nightmare on you that wears out batteries every 30 minutes.

62

Above all, you must depend upon the reputation of the manufacturer...the record a company has achieved over the years. It has happened many times that a detector with a square foot of printed circuit board was out-performed by a detector with a board the size of a playing card. And, think of what it may cost you to have that one square foot of printed circuit board repaired! Knowledgeable and conscientious engineers continually strive to design circuitry with minimum components. The more components there are, the less reliable the product. And, *nothing* does the work of a microprocessor in a detector except a microprocessor.

From my earliest days as a metal detector manufacturer I have said that there is no one particular brand or type of detector that is "just perfect" or that will do every job perfectly with total capabilities. Now that I've hunted with our new Grand Master Hunter CX III, with notch discrimination, a true non-motion All Metal mode and *TreasureTalk*, I must question myself on this statement!

Nevertheless, there can be no argument that a number of detectors are available today in all price ranges that will perform admirably in many situations and under extreme environmental conditions, and a few detectors (particularly the one mentioned above) will do most jobs quite satisfactorily.

If possible, rent a detector of the type you wish to buy. Spend as many hours as possible using that detector to learn its characteristics and capabilities. There is no better way to find out for yourself if a detector is suited for you, than to use one. Many dealers have rental programs, and the few dollars that you spend on rental fees can often be repaid by the detector many times over. Some rental contracts specify that a portion of, or all, rental fees can be used toward the purchase of a new detector.

What should such a *capable* metal detector — one that will find treasure — cost? Answering a question with a question, I might respond, "What should a car cost?" The answers to both questions are the same. The price will depend on the quality of the product and the features (options) it offers. And it is probably more important to rely on a dependable dealer when purchasing a detector than when buying a car.

All of the major detector manufacturers generally offer a wide selection of instruments, varying both in price and ability. As a rule of thumb, however, it would be well *never* to consider any detector you can purchase for less than $150 to $175 (early 1993 prices).

No matter what their cost, all detectors are designed to find coins...the vast majority of hobbyists seek little more. Some instruments are intended principally to find coins, with others developed specifically for different hunting tasks.

Concerning dollars and cents, please don't make the very common mistake of thinking that if you look around and choose the highest priced detector, you will be getting the best instrument. Instead, determine a price *range* that fits your pocketbook. Then, diligently analyze all detectors priced within that range before buying the one that you believe suits you best.

Let's say that you've decided to spend $500 (from $450 to $550) on a new detector. Analyze and use the various models in that range. Compare them and judge their versatility, capability, quality and the ability to do the specific jobs you require. Then, purchase the detector that you find best suited to your metal detection wants and needs.

Be sure to take a look at the detector. Does it look like quality? Does it have jagged edges or unfinished parts? Is it ruggedly built or does the control housing flop on its handle? Pick up the detector and handle it. Does it feel like quality? Grasp the control housing and rock it back and forth. Is it solid or loose? Switch on the detector and put it through its paces by adjusting any controls.

Speaking of controls, just how many are there? You go into the field to find treasure, not to prove your expertise by manipulating controls on an electronic instrument. Are all controls absolutely necessary? Are they smooth to operate? When you test the detector by scanning it over various targets, does it respond smoothly or are there sudden changes and squawks and squeals in the audio?

Please don't rely too much on the results of so-called "air tests," i.e., checking the distance that a detector will detect various small and large targets with nothing but air between the searchcoil and target. Of course, you'll probably want to check a detector's sensitivity for yourself in such a test. If so, try to measure detection distance with a small coin like a penny. Don't use a silver dollar! The smaller coin is a better test target. If a detector will pick up a penny to a good distance, it will surely detect a silver dollar to an even greater one.

Let me point out, however, that the new computerized detectors have made "air tests" completely invalid.

Remember that microprocessor-controlled circuitry enables a detector to analyze simultaneously all soil conditions as well as the target(s) beneath its searchcoil. Thus, computerized detectors with microprocessor controls, when properly designed, can sometimes detect objects at greater distances (depths) in the ground than in the air! It's a fact.

Selection Checkpoints

When selecting a metal detector, here are a few specific points to consider:

- **Portability.**
  - When not in use, the equipment may be quickly and easily disassembled, without tools, for storage in a protective case.
- **Ease of Operation.**
  - The equipment should be lightweight and engineered for comfortable use over extended periods of time. Remember, however, that the lightest equipment may not be sufficiently durable.
  - The equipment must have certain controls and functions to be effective, but it should have only those controls and functions necessary to do the job intended.
  - Extra controls and functions can confuse an operator, especially one who uses the equipment only occasionally. Complicated adjustment requirements limit the effectiveness of a search...and make a hunt less enjoyable. Furthermore,

unnecessary controls and functions require extra circuitry which can degrade reliability and wear out batteries.

- **Basic controls:**
  - Circuit or means to check the batteries. Access to batteries (if not rechargeable) should be easy. Are the batteries readily available and reasonably priced?
  - Push button or automatic controls to switch easily between different hunting modes (All Metal and Discriminate, for example).
  - Compatibility with different sizes and types of searchcoils. No matter what you are told, one "standard" searchcoil will not be sufficient...especially after you gain expertise. Make certain your detector will accept other sizes and types...and that they are available!

- **Capability.**
  - The detector should be capable of performing, with good efficiency, all the tasks you intend for it to perform.
  - Necessary searchcoils (see above) and other accessories should be standard equipment or available for optional purchase.

- **Depth Detection.**
  - When evaluating a metal detector, depth detection – the ability to detect an object at a given distance – is sometimes the only point a purchaser considers. True, this is vitally important. But, a quality detector should also have excellent sensitivity, mechanical and electrical stability, plus the ability to operate at great efficiency over *any* type of mineralized ground. Without all these characteristics, you may have an inadequate metal detector.
  - When evaluating sensitivity, evaluate different types of objects. Some instruments are more sensitive to iron, some are less sensitive to coins. Detection depth, however, can be reduced when operated in the Discriminate mode. So, make sure that not much detection depth is lost when discrimination is dialed in.

- **Durability** is important because a metal detector will often be used many hours in rugged environments. Since electronic circuits can be expected to be functional for many years, a strong mechanical package is important:

- · **– Appearance!**

This concerns *your* durability because you're probably going to "live" with this detector for many years. Will you be proud to be seen with it? A "little tin box" may be just the thing for storing coins and keepsakes, but do you really want to carry around a detector that features one?

– Metal structural components should be strong enough to prevent excessive flexing. Flexing can cause metal fatigue and breakage and be a source of mechanical instability.

– Rivets, screws and other fastening devices must do their job dependably to prevent loosening of the mechanical package due to use.

– Plastic parts should be properly designed and manufactured from the materials that prevent breakage, warping, melting and cracking from heat and cold.

– If the detector's housing is metallic with sharp corners, make certain they're not sharp enough to tear your clothing or car seats or to scratch walls and furniture.

– Properly designed carrying cases should be available to protect the equipment during transportation and storage.

- · **Environmental Considerations.**

– Moisture protection is important to enable the equipment to be used in light rain or among wet vegetation.

– Submersible searchcoils allow searches in shallow water as well as under conditions listed above.

– If the equipment is to be used under water or is to be used extensively in shallow water, a guaranteed seal is absolutely necessary.

– A sealed underwater detector may be necessary (it's certainly desirable) for a salt beach environment to eliminate the effects of sand, moisture and the corrosive atmosphere on the circuitry, controls, and metal surfaces.

Evaluation Summation

When evaluating a specific detector, here is a summary of things to look for...questions you *should* ask:

• Is the detector easy to operate? How much "adjustment" is *really* necessary?

• When the detector is not used for an extended period, is it so complicated that you won't remember how to use it?

• Are the instrument and its components well protected for storage, transportation and use?

• Is the detector easily assembled and are the batteries and all controls readily accessible and properly located?

• Is the equipment designed so that weight is always properly balanced?

• Are desired searchcoils and other accessories available? Can all searchcoils be submerged?

• Are controls clearly marked? Is the instruction manual adequate, yet easy to understand?

• Is the equipment designed to do the jobs intended? Is it suitable for the operating environments in which it will be used?

Determining Capability

This is a basic selection guide to help you choose the correct, or optimum detector for *your* use. Various detector characteristics, including ground balance and discrimination for the type of searching you will be doing, are discussed. It is divided into three categories:

• Treasure Hunting for coin, cache and relics (also see Chapters 8-11),

• Water Hunting (see Chapters 12-14),

• Gold Hunting (see Chapters 15-16).

There are numerous books written which describe the various facets of metal detecting in much greater detail. *Modern Metal Detectors, The New Successful Coin Hunting, Treasure Recovery from Sand and Sea* and *Modern Electronic Prospecting,* all published by Ram Publishing Company, are recommended. To improve your expertise and to become more proficient in every phase of detector use you should read these books, as well as others on the hobby.

Your selection and purchase of a metal detector ought to have the same careful consideration that goes with anything you buy. Shopping has become very much a part of life, and you must depend upon yourself to make the right choice. The more clearly you understand what you want, the more likely you are to be correct in your choice. Choosing a metal detector should take no less time and consideration than buying any other valuable and expensive item. Buying the correct instrument depends both on whether you understand all the important facts about the different types and what your requirements really are.

In the following section, I list most of the facets of metal detector usage; and I recommend the type instrument or instruments and searchcoils to use. I describe operational aspects so that you can compare the features and capabilities of the various brands and types. This information is designed to recommend a specific *type* of detector, not a brand or a model. Instructions on using that detector will be found in Chapters 8 through 15. I hope this information will help you decide if the metal detector you are thinking of buying will, indeed, do the job you intend for it to do.

Coin Hunting

At Garrett we recognize that every detector that we manufacture will be used, at least part of the time, to hunt coins...and, many detectors will be used for nothing else! Thus, *every* detector should be manufactured with coin hunting in mind. Discrimination control is a must for coin hunting detectors. Also, the instruments must be ground balanced. Ideally, you should have precise, notch discrimination control to help you avoid unwanted targets.

Round searchcoils eight to nine inches in diameter have traditionally been preferred for coin hunting. This size is lightweight and has good depth detection and scanning width. Something new, however, has come into the picture...elliptical searchcoils. These newly designed coils provide good scanning width and have proved especially effective in areas where trash metal targets abound.

For deeper penetration, use the 10- or 12-inch sizes. Pinpointing will be a little more difficult with larger searchcoils, but you can expect to get the deeper coins. For operation in tight places adjacent to sidewalks, metal buildings and fences, and for Super-Sniping, use a three-to-four-inch diameter searchcoil.

Cache or Money Hunting

Ground balancing is essential, and you should choose a manual-adjust instrument with a *true* non-motion All Metal mode. It should be capable of using a large searchcoil and the Depth Multiplier. The Bloodhound Depth Multiplier should be used whenever possible because it detects deeply and ignores small metallic objects like nails, bits of wire, etc.

Since you are not looking for small objects, forget small coils. A 10-inch size might be good, but a 12-inch size would be even better. When using large searchcoils, an armrest or hipmount configuration is recommended. Is one available for the model you select?

Relic Hunting

Relic hunting calls for the same type of equipment as cache hunting. You definitely need large searchcoils, and you may need a good hipmount configuration. Most hunters do not use any form of discrimination because they don't want to take the chance of missing valuable iron relics. Some use a small amount of discrimination only when searching for brass and lead objects.

Ghost Town Searching

If you are outdoors and looking for coins, rings and jewelry, any quality detector with good discrimination will give the best results. Since most ghost towns contain many junk metal targets, discrimination will be important. Oftentimes, a great amount of junk may necessitate your reducing the sensitivity (detection depth) of your detector.

If you are searching for ghost town relics or money caches, however, you'll need an instrument with a true non-motion All Metal mode that can be manually ground balanced. It would be best to use the largest searchcoil you have available. Large money caches may be quite deep, so you should consider using the Bloodhound Depth Multiplier attachment. This multiplies a detector's depth capability, producing great depth on objects larger than quart size while almost completely ignoring nails and other small metal trash.

Indoors, the same rules apply in ghost towns as in all other forms of indoor searching.

Hunting Near or In Water

Several good new detectors have been developed primarily for water hunting. These instruments feature automatic ground balance and offer excellent discrimination capabilities. Another type detector to use when searching ocean beaches is a pulse induction type with discrimination. To search fresh water beaches, most any type of quality detector will be more or less suitable.

There is a phenomenon that causes pulse induction detectors to detect coins and rings extremely deep in salt water. Consequently, immediately after they were first placed on the market, they became a favorite among beach coin hunters, especially those who search ocean beaches.

When hunting on any beach, be sure to wear headphones for maximum depth detection and elimination of surf noise.

There are two basic mechanical configurations for detectors designed for use deep under the water. Primarily for underwater searching, one type has the searchcoil and housing permanently attached to a short stem. The stem is too short to use above water, but accessories are available for converting long-stem land units to the short stem arrangement for underwater use.

Some underwater detectors use meters and lights. Indicator lights are not as sensitive as meter indicators, which are very sensitive but are difficult to watch at all times and, in all but clear water, become difficult to see.

Gold Hunting

The recommended type detector for gold hunting will have excellent ground balance and precise calibrated discrimination. The ideal type is an instrument with a true non-motion All Metal mode. It should be capable of manual ground balancing and it should have been proven in the field. Not all detectors are the same! Some are more versatile and sensitive than others and some are more capable of operating over highly mineralized ground.

Let me suggest that before you purchase a gold hunting detector, you consider just how much of your time will be spent searching for gold. Then, consider how effective your detector will be for other types of hunting. A detector without a Discriminate mode, for example, will rarely be satisfactory for coin hunting. You may decide on a gold hunting detector that will also be effective for other types of THing.

Always select a model that offers a wide range of searchcoils. Selection of the right searchcoil depends, to a great extent, upon how well you have mastered your detector. Then, how well you apply your experiences and observations will in large measure determine your success.

The Bloodhound Depth Multiplier attachment will substantially increase the depth to which you can detect large ore veins, even those containing iron ore. Such iron ore, when in association with gold and silver, can even enhance the detection characteristics of veins.

Finally, no matter what type or brand of detector you buy, remember my earlier advice. Always try to buy one just a *little better* than you intended. As you come to love your detector over the years, you'll be glad you did!

7 – How To Find Treasure...

Searching

As long as it performs basic functions, a poorly built detector will produce more in the hands of an experienced THer than a high quality detector will in the hands of a person who does not understand the instrument or know how to use it. Some detectors will barely detect a coin one inch deep, yet others will detect that same coin at extreme depths. A most important factor, however, in successful detector operation is the expertise and ability of the operator.

This book is designed for all THers, but this chapter is for metal detector operators...especially those relatively new to the hobby. It contains practical methods, tips and procedures recommended to all who use a metal detector. It is my sincere hope that study of this chapter along with others in this book will enable each of you to increase your THing abilities. The success you obtain will be in direct proportion to the amount of time and study that you devote to the hobby.

Metal detector manufacturers get letters from customers who complain about finding nothing but bottlecaps with their detector. Yet, other letters seem to bubble over with enthusiasm and joy because the writers are finding coins, rings, jewelry and other valuables — and finding them *with the very same detectors*. Accompanying photographs often offer further testimony to the tremendous quantities of treasure they have found.

What is the difference? Certainly, it doesn't lie in the capability of the detector. One can obviously take identical instruments and place them in the hands of two different people with entirely different results.

The best advice I can give you about any metal detector is perhaps the most obvious. *Read your instruction manual!* Yes, that's right...carefully read and study the operator's manual that accompanied your detector. In fact, we at Garrett recommend that you study this manual *before* you purchase a detector. If the manufacturer has "skimped" on providing instructions and advice, you might find yourself shorted in other areas of an instrument.

On the other hand, an extremely detailed manual that you find hard to understand could well indicate a detector that's going to prove complicated and difficult to learn how to use. At Garrett we believe that our computerized, microprocessor-controlled detectors should be *simple to use*, not difficult. Our *Owner's Manuals* will tell you this. If some other manual indicates otherwise, be wary of the detector it describes.

Getting Started

If you buy through the mail, or from someone who won't or can't offer instruction, you must work especially hard to learn about your detector. Not learning your instrument properly will probably cause you to miss far more treasure than the dollars you saved by ordering from the cheapest source. Your goal should be to find treasure...not a metal detector bargain!

Getting hands-on instructions from the dealer from whom you purchased your new detector is the first step. This step cannot be stressed too greatly. Learn all you can from your dealer, then – after you have studied your instruction manual (and audio/video tapes) thoroughly – go into the field with a notebook and carefully write down all questions you have and the problems that have arisen. Return to the dealer for your answers. Don't neglect this vital first step! If the dealer can't answer your questions, write or call the manufacturer!

Assuming that you have read this book carefully and made a thorough study of the metal detector market to select the best instrument for you, the next step is to make up your mind that you are going to learn how to use this detector properly, regardless of the time and effort it takes. Never deviate from your decision! A detector will remove the blindfold and permit you to "see" coins, jewelry and other buried and concealed valuables. But you have to trust your detector. You have to learn the correct methods of operating it. You have to learn its idiosyncrasies. You have to learn what makes it tick! In other words...

Learn your metal detector!

Don't worry — at least at first — about what you are finding. As you put miles behind your searchcoil, you will find yourself getting better and better with your detector. You will become more at ease in using it, and there will be fewer and fewer "problems" that bother you. The quantity of found items will be growing at an accelerated rate. All though your learning and training period and even on down through the years, you must develop persistence. *Never give up!* Persistence, Persistence, **Persistence**! These are the words of a successful operator, the late L.L. "Abe" Lincoln.

When you begin your home study, don't immediately assemble the detector and run outside to begin looking for treasure. First, read your instruction manual...not once, but several times. The first time through, read it as you would a novel — from front to back without stopping. You should pay no attention to the metal detector or its controls. Simply read the instruction manual. If video or audio instruction tapes are available for your detector, watch or listen to these several times. Then, assemble your instrument according to the instructions on the tapes or in the manual. Take the time to do it right.

The next step is to become familiar with your instrument's controls as you begin to operate the detector in its various modes and functions. The instruction manual and tape(s) should guide you through this learning process and enable you to start practicing with your detector.

Lay it on a wooden bench or table. Do not use a table with metal legs and braces because the metal could interfere with your testing. Begin with the part of your instruction manual that describes detection of metal. Go through the procedure!

If your detector is equipped with a sensitivity or detection depth control, test the detector at several levels. Test the instrument with various metal targets. After you have become familiar with the sounds of your instrument, its LCD or meter and its response to various targets in various modes, it is time to go out into the field.

You'll now be *so* grateful for all the knowledge you gained indoors. When you worked with your detector on a table, operation was probably very simple. Now that you are outside, the situation has changed. If you change a pre-set threshold with the searchcoil held in the air, when you lower the searchcoil to the ground, you may be in for a surprise. As you lower the coil, the audio sound may begin to change with the meter deflecting up or down because of minerals or metal targets in the ground where you are standing. It will be necessary for you to learn exactly what is causing any signal changes.

The beginner should initially consider any Discrimination controls as "set and forget." If your detector has a dial, set it to zero discrimination (All-Metal detection) and leave it there until you have at least 10 hours operating time. In other words, dig everything!

We have developed "Starter Phases" for our new computerized Garrett detectors. These instruments are so simple to operate that you can press just one touchpad and begin hunting successfully — with absolutely no adjustments necessary. We urge all customers to follow the instructions of the "Starter Phase," no matter how much experience they have with a metal detector.

The following exercises will be helpful in learning how to use a metal detector while gaining confidence in its abilities.

Note gold pan that this treasure hunter (using headphones) will employ to help him scoop up and examine any targets found in this pile of rocks.

No short course, however, can ever substitute for study, application and continual practice. These instructions are for computerized models with "one-touchpad" operation but will also apply to the familiar and popular motion detector with automatic ground balance.

1. Read carefully the instruction manual accompanying the detector; read it again; study it.

2. Follow instructions to assemble the detector, using the smallest diameter searchcoil, if more than one is available.

3. As instructed in the instruction manual, set any necessary dials to "Preset Points" specified on the detector's controls. Make *only* those adjustments that are required.

4. Hold the detector with the searchcoil about three feet off the ground. Turn the detector on.

5. With detectors that feature automatic threshold adjustment use the level already set in the detector. If the detector requires adjustment, set the audio control to shut out all sound, then increase it slowly until just a faint sound is heard. This is called threshold level.

6. Lower the searchcoil to a height of about two inches above the ground and begin scanning.

8. When the sound increases and/or an indication is shown on the meter or LCD panel, a target is buried in the ground below the searchcoil.

When a treasure hunter is scanning his searchcoil over the ground or in the water, a detector reports information on targets in three ways:

• Increases or decreases in audible volume (universal on all detectors);

• Graphic information presented on LCD meters (sometimes reported in a numerical "code").

This treasure hunter is using a probe to help recover his target with as little damange as possible to the well manicured sod where he is hunting.

• Meter deflections (types of meters can vary greatly, along with the amount and accuracy of the information they present);

Acceptable objects cause the audio or visual indicators to increase in amplitude; unacceptable objects cause the indicators to decrease. Metered target identification indicators can provide additional information concerning the possible "value" of targets.

Techniques of scanning for treasure with a metal detector are many and varied. Here are some simple recommendations:

• Set the volume control to a minimum threshold level. If silent operation is desired, always make certain that such operation is just below an audible level. I personally never use silent audio since it is possible to overlook "fringe" signals and miss targets.

• Never dial in more discrimination than you need; too much may reduce detection capability.

• Run-down batteries are by far the single most common source of detector "failure;" be sure to check your batteries before venturing out, and carry spare batteries whenever you are searching.

• Keep the searchcoil level as you scan and always scan slowly and methodically; scan the searchcoil from side to side and in a straight line in front of you.

• Do not scan the searchcoil in an arc unless the arc width is narrow (about two feet) or unless you are scanning extremely slowly. The straight-line scan method allows you to cover more ground width in each sweep and permits you to keep the searchcoil level throughout each sweep. This method reduces skipping and helps you overlap more uniformly.

• Overlap by advancing the searchcoil as much as 50% of the coil's diameter at the end of each sweep path. Occasionally scan an area from a different angle. Do not raise the searchcoil above scanning level at the end of each sweep. When the searchcoil begins to reach the extremes of each sweep, you will find yourself rotating your upper body to stretch out for an even wider sweep. This gives the double benefit of scanning a wider sweep and gaining additional exercise. To insure that you completely scan any given area, use string or cord to mark scan paths three to six feet wide.

• You can learn to use a probe to locate the exact spot where coins are buried; this will help you retrieve coins with minimum damage to grass and the target.

• Always fill in your hole after you dig a target; holes are not only unsightly, but they can be dangerous. Before filling a hole, however, be sure to check it again with your detector to make certain you have recovered everything in and around it. It's embarrassing to have someone recover a target from a hole you originally dug. I know; it's happened to me!

During the learning phase with your own detector, keep in mind that you should work smarter, not harder. Each time you receive a signal — before you dig — try to guess what the target is, what size it is, its shape and its depth. Analyze the audio and/or meter signals. Say to yourself, "This is a coin," or "This is a bottlecap. It is about three inches deep." Then pay careful attention when you dig the object. Try to determine exactly how deep it is and how it was lying in the ground.

Did you guess right? Great! If not, try to determine why. The more you do this, the greater your success will be. You will quickly learn how to use and actually "read" your instrument and understand everything it is telling you.

As you scan the searchcoil over the ground, scan at a rate of about one foot per second. Don't get in a hurry, and don't try to cover an acre in 10 minutes. Always remember that what you are looking for is buried just below the sweep you are now making with your searchcoil. It's not across the field.

After you have used your detector for several hours, you can begin to test its discrimination. Study your owner's manual. But, whatever you do, don't use too much discrimination...just enough to eliminate from detection the junk you have been digging. Do not try to set the control to eliminate pulltabs. That can come later when you know more about your detector and only when you feel such discrimination is absolutely necessary.

If you haven't started using headphones, now is the time to do so. You'll learn how important they really are. You'll dig coins that you couldn't detect just by listening to a detector's speaker. You'll hear sounds you didn't hear before. Headphones may get hot and the cord may get in your way but the rewards will make it all worthwhile.

After you have even more experience and are beginning to get comfortable with your detector, it's time to go back over the same areas you searched before you learned how to use your machine. You'll surprised at the quantity of coins and other objects you missed. In fact, each time you come back to these places you'll find more coins and other treasures, especially at greater depths.

Always remember that well designed detectors are not complicated or difficult to learn to use. The first time you drove a car it was difficult, but now you drive without thinking about it. The same will be true with your detector. Take it easy, and don't give up if you think it is not performing as it should. Just keep working with your detector, restudy your manual, contact your dealer or manufacturer, and ask for more information. Quite often, problems are cleared up with just one simple demonstration by your dealer or someone who knows how to use detectors. Remember, keep the Detection Depth (Sensitivity) control turned to a low level and certainly not above its "Initial Set Point." Scan with the searchcoil about two inches above the ground and scan at a moderate speed. Even in areas with large amounts of "junk" metal, which are very difficult to work, reduced detection depth and moderate scanning speed let you hear individual target signals rather than just a jumbled mass of sounds.

Success stories are written every day. A lot of treasure is being found and a lot of treasure is waiting to be found where you live. Detectors are not magic wands, but when used correctly they will locate buried and concealed treasure. Keep your faith in your detector, have patience and continue using your instrument until you have it mastered. Success will be yours!

Make Your Own Test Plot

One of the first things a new detector owner does is bury a few coins to see how deeply they can be detected. The usual result...*disappointment.* You see, newly buried coins are quite difficult to detect. The longer an object has been buried, the easier it can be detected. Not only is a "barrier" to electromagnetic field penetration created when a coin is first buried, but no "halo effect" has been developed. As time passes, coins become more closely associated, electrically, with surrounding earth materials and the molecules of metal begin to leave and move out into the surrounding soil. Also, it is theorized that in some cases (especially in salt water) the coin's surface becomes a better conductor. In some areas it is believed that coins buried for some time can be detected at twice the depth compared with coins that have just been buried.

Select an area for your own test plot. First, scan the area very thoroughly with no discrimination and remove all metal from the ground. Select targets such as various coins, a bottlecap, a nail and a pulltab. Select also a pint jar filled with scrap copper and/or aluminum metal, a long object such as a foot-long pipe and a large object such as a gallon can. Bury all these objects about three feet apart, in rows, and make a map showing where each item is buried and note its depth.

Bury pennies at varying depths, beginning at one inch. Continue, with the deepest buried about six inches deep. Bury one at about two inches but stand it on edge. Bury a penny at about two inches with a bottlecap about four inches off to one side. Bury the bottlecap, nail and pulltab separately about two inches deep. Bury the jar at twelve inches to the top of its lid. Bury the pipe horizontally three or four inches deep. Bury the gallon can with the lid two feet below the surface.

The purpose of the buried coins is to familiarize you with the sound of money. If you can't detect the deeper coins, don't worry. After a while, you'll be able to detect them quickly. If you can detect everything in your test plot, rebury some items deeper. The penny buried next to the bottle cap can give you experience in Super Sniping with a smaller searchcoil and will help you learn to distinguish individual objects. The jar and gallon can will help you learn to recognize "dull" sounds of large, deeply buried objects. The pipe will help you learn to contour. Check the targets with and without headphones. You'll be amazed at the difference headphones make.

The test plot is important. Don't neglect it. From time to time expand it, rebury the targets deeper and add new ones. Your test plot is important because your success in scanning over it will be a measure of how well you are progressing and how well you have learned your equipment. Remember, however, that you must make an accurate map and keep it up to date when you change and/or add to your test plot.

Miscellaneous Tips

When searching areas adjacent to wire fences, metal buildings, metal parking meter posts, etc., reduce detection depth and scan the searchcoil parallel to the structure. This lets you get as close to it as possible.

Coins lying in the ground at an angle may be missed on one searchcoil pass but detected when the searchcoil approaches from a different angle. If your detector has a volume control, keep it set at maximum. Don't confuse volume control with audio (threshold) control. You should use earphones that have individual earphone volume adjustment and set each one to suit yourself.

If you are working on the beach, set discrimination at about bottlecap rejection. A slight amount of adjusting may be necessary but you can set the detector to ignore salt water. Pulse Induction detectors and others designed for beach hunting ignore salt water automatically.

Use your common sense. *Think* your way through perplexing situations. Remember, success comes from detector expertise, research, patience, enthusiasm and using common sense.

Don't expect to find tons of treasure every time you go out! In fact, there may be times when you don't find anything. But the hobby's real joy and the reward of detecting is never knowing what you'll dig up next!

84

Coin Hunting

H unting for coins is the heart and soul of the treasure hunting hobby...especially for those THers with metal detectors. Literally everybody hunts for coins. They are certainly the initial target that most first-time detector owners seek. But, why do so many people hunt for coins?

Because they are "there!"

Think of the countless millions of coins in use today. Where are they? In the cash boxes of businesses, large and small...in the drawers and vaults of banks and money-changing institutions...in private collections and museums...in the coin purses and "piggy banks" of millions of individuals. The total number of *all* these coins truly boggles the mind. Imagine them together in one place...all piled in your yard or in a nearby park? Why, this mountain of precious metal would rise higher than a tall building!

Yet, the number of *lost* coins far exceeds the total in circulation today. That's right, all of the lost coins – now lying on or beneath the ground, hidden in houses and buildings or in waters of lakes, streams and oceans – would rise far above that mountain you just imagined in your yard. Coins just awaiting discovery – "finders keepers" coins that belong to the first person to find them or dig them up – exceed in number and *far surpass in value* all the coins currently in commerce, savings and collections.

Where are they, you ask? Where are these lost coins that are just waiting to be found? Literally all over the world. Except perhaps for the polar icecaps and barren Asian mountain peaks, I sincerely believe that there is no place on the face of the earth where coins cannot be found, usually in abundance. And, by the way, I'm not too sure that polar explorers and Himalayan mountain climbers always brought back every coin they started with.

Literally multitudes of coins can be found everywhere. You just have to look for them.

This chapter can serve as your introduction to the fascinating and rewarding hobby of searching for coins...with or without a metal detector. Let me warn you, however, that you'll soon find yourself "hooked." After you begin finding coins — and especially when you make that first "big" find — coin-hunting will be ever on your mind. No matter where you are or what you are doing, you'll find yourself subconsciously evaluating the coin-hunting prospects of that location. And, if you don't have a metal detector...you'll soon find yourself wanting — and, acquiring — one!

And, you know what? You'll love it!

At Garrett we know that every metal detector we design and build will be used at one time or another to search for coins. We also suspect that many of our detectors will be used for no other purpose. Oh, jewelry and other valuable items will certainly be sought, but it will be coins that are the thrust of the search for most hobbyists, no matter what their intentions.

Thus, it is essential that any detector hobbyist master coin-hunting techniques which will be used in all other forms of THing.

The recommended detector for hunting coins is a modern instrument with automatic ground balancing and good discrimination. The best instruments, however, are the new computerized detectors with microprocessor controls that provide alternatives between several modes and discrimination levels. Of course, any detector with an All Metal mode will find more and deeper coins, but every target should be dug. This can be a blessing in disguise, since valuable metal objects are sometimes rejected when discrimination is used.

Coin hunting is a field in which you can especially excel with an Ultra GTA, the Grand Master Hunter CX II or III or the Master Hunter CX...Garrett's computerized detectors with microprocessor controls! Any of these versatile instruments will be found especially fitted for coin hunting.

Consider the Ultra GTA. Although they have universal capabilities, Ultra GTA detectors were designed primarily as coin hunters. The greater depth and precise discrimination possible with microprocessor-controlled circuitry combine with the GTA's light weight and ease of handling to make it a superb instrument for finding coins.

Whether you choose to hunt for coins in a park or on a beach, the GTA's *Coins* operating mode (or *Mode B*) will offer discrimination that responds ideally to conditions normally encountered. This discrimination preset in the *Coins* and *B* modes is designed to eliminate detection of lower conductivity trash targets normally encountered in coin hunting, such as bottlecaps and most pulltabs.

Another equipment tip is one we've already discussed. Let me urge you again, however, always to use headphones. Get a quality set and you'll be amazed at how much more you can hear from your detector. With a modern instrument that tries to tell you such a great deal, you really want to be able to listen to it.

When using headphones (or, even the speaker, if you must) we urge that you operate with audio threshold at a very slight level of sound. Adjust it for the faintest sound you can hear.

Some treasure hunters can find targets with silent operation, true; but it has also been proven that silent operation results in a slight loss of depth. You will also lose some ability to read all targets properly, especially in trashy areas.

Coins & Junk

No matter what threshold you use, there will be times when you hear a coin tone while scanning over a spot in one direction and a standard audio blip when scanning from another angle. This is most likely a junk target; however, we advise you not just to walk away from it. Continue scanning back and forth across it from numerous angles. Draw your imaginary "X;" slide your searchcoil from side to side. Even push it forward and backward. Listen to the sound carefully. If you ever get the coin tone in both directions (headphones are a real help here), dig the target. You'll probably find a coin in close proximity to some sort of junk.

We know how much will power it takes to resist the blips coming over your headphones or from the audio speaker beneath the armrest of your GTA 1000. You know a target exists, and it's human nature to want to dig them all! Remember, however, that a quality modern detector will never lie to you. Its LCD display or meter and audible sounds will properly identify all objects being detected beneath the searchcoil at any given instant.

Scanning speed is very important. Your detector will operate and analyze targets no matter what speed you swing the searchcoil. We recommend that you operate at a speed of between one to two feet per second. Go even slower, and you might be surprised at your increased success, especially in areas with lots of junk targets. We suggest that you try a test. Slow down and scan with your searchcoil very deliberately. You may reap great benefits.

Some of you prefer to scan with a searchcoil lightly skimming the ground. This is fine; don't worry about it. Our only recommendation about such activity is that you use the appropriate skid plate (coil cover) to protect your searchcoil against unnecessary abrasion and wear.

I recommend that coin hunters use the "standard" (8 1/2-inch) searchcoil for scanning most parks, playgrounds, beaches and other conventional coin hunting areas. It is the best general purpose, all-around searchcoil. Numerous letters and personal inquiries regularly ask me about use of the larger coils. My answer is a definite *yes*...the reason being that larger coils can detect deeper and find even the smallest coins.

Now, those of you to whom this is a new idea may be asking just when should you use the larger searchcoil. Good question!

After you scan an area with the 8 1/2-inch coil, you may suspect that you are encountering deep targets that give you only a faint signal, even with headphones. If so, you're detecting at the outer limits of that all-purpose searchcoil, and you may be missing deeper coins. You need the additional detection depth that's available with the 12 1/2-inch searchcoil. After scanning such an area thoroughly with the 8 1/2-inch searchcoil, go over it again with the larger coil, scanning very slowly and using headphones. If there are deeper coins to be found, you'll detect them!

Smaller searchcoils will make you more efficient in your coin hunting efforts. You will dig a higher ratio of coins to trash, but detection depth will not be as great as with 8 to 12-inch sizes. Smaller and larger coils should definitely be weapons in your normal coin hunting arsenal.

For instance, if a park is known as a good coin producer, but has been overworked, you may want to consider a larger searchcoil. Adjust Discrimination controls to reject typical trash found in the area or set it to "zero." Adjust the detector to ignore iron mineralization and use one of the pinpointing methods explained in this book. As you retrieve coins and trash, notice their depth. If mostly junk is found in the first few inches, you may want to dig only the deeper targets.

If your detector is equipped with a depth measuring meter, dig only the targets beyond a predetermined depth. If yours is equipped with a detection depth control, try setting it to maximum. When you have pinpointed an object, rotate the control to minimum and recheck the target. If you don't detect it now, dig. It will be deep. You should analyze detector operation using various detection depth control settings to find the optimum setting for any particular coin area.

New elliptical coils are now becoming increasingly popular for several reasons. A 5x10-inch coil offers an effective 10-inch scanning path, yet is lighter than a normal 10-inch coil. The new 2D elliptical coils also offer additional depth and are useful in trashy areas since they scan only in the small area down the center of the searchcoil.

Fourteen-inch searchcoils can be used for coin hunting and are surprisingly sensitive to small coins. You may find pinpointing more difficult at first, but extra depth can be achieved.

If you're new to THing, you may be getting somewhat skeptical about all this enthusiasm. You may even be questioning your potential as a coin hunter. Honestly, aren't you perhaps wondering just how many coins are *really* lost? And, you may also wonder if it will actually *pay* you to spend your valuable time hunting them. You may wonder too if you'll get anything more out this new hobby than fresh air and exercise – which many people, incidentally, might consider enough!

Where Do I Look?

First of all, we must always search for coins *where* they have been lost, and we must always search with the *proper* equipment.

But, where to look is easy! Anywhere people have been – which is practically everywhere. Once you get really interested in this hobby, you'll soon have the problem of so many places to search that you truly won't know where to go next. The next few pages of this chapter will list locations where coins might be found. At first glance, you'll think the list somewhat lengthy and certainly all-encompassing.

But, don't rush, please. I urge that you study this list, try to recall personal experiences over the years and keep your mind open to all the additional locations where you might find lost coins. Believe me, this list should suggest a lot of them to you:

Where People Live(d)

Indoors

Closets and shelves.

In the walls.

Above and beneath door and window sills.

Underneath or along baseboards.

Underneath or along edges of linoleum or other flooring...especially adjacent to holes.

Garages and storage sheds.

Outbuildings, such as barns and animal shelters.

Crawl spaces under structures.

Outdoors

Your own yard.

Driveways and parking areas...where people would have gotten out of cars or carriages.

Doorways...where coins might have been spilled.

Next to porches and steps...where people might have sat.

Porch and step railings...where children might have played.

Around and along all walkways and paths.

Around old outbuildings...on the ground where they stand (or stood) and along the path to the house.

Around hitching posts and hitching post racks.

Between gate posts.

Near mail boxes. Remember that in rural areas people used to put coins in the mailbox, along with the letters to be picked up by carriers. Often, some of these coins would spill when pulled out by the postman. I've heard tales of coin hunters finding Indian head pennies and other old coins around the locations of rural mail boxes that haven't been used for years.

Well and pump sites.

Storm cellar and basement entrances.

Around watering troughs.

Along fence rows and around stiles.

Under large trees...children could have played or had swings here..."shade tree mechanics" might have worked here...especially look for trees with adjacent built-in benches.

Under clotheslines or places where they might have been.

Around patios and garden furniture areas...look here, also, for permanently installed benches and seating areas.

Where People Play(ed)

Fishing piers, boat ramps and landings.

Ferryboat loading and unloading sites.

Fishing camps and health resorts ("watering" places).

Abandoned resort areas.

Horse and hiking trails...especially spots where people may have stopped to rest or camp.

Swimming pools or "holes"...especially abandoned or old ones.

Children's camps...especially concession or play areas.

Around ski tow loading and unloading areas.

Beach swimming areas.

Miniature golf courses...driving range tees.

Shooting and target ranges (but, expect to find lots of shell casings).

Old springs or wishing wells.

Pioneer campgrounds.

River fords.

Bluffs and embankments that might have served as playground "slides."

Abandoned trailer parks.

Beneath stadium seats.

Bandstands, gazebos, entertainment platforms...or where they once stood.

Amusement parks, fairgrounds, carnival and circus sites...the potential here is unbelievable.

Rodeo grounds...today's and those of the past.

Old horse-racing tracks and spectator areas.

Parks...and let your imagination run wild...benches, drinking fountains, large trees, steps, picnic tables, sports areas, walkways...this list could go on and on.

Drive-in theater locations...around concession areas or where children might have played...around ticket windows.

Motels...current and abandoned locations...recreation areas and concession machines.

Historical markers and highway locations that have maps or that present good photographic possibilities.

Tourist Spots

Just thinking about historical markers and the roadside parks where tourists and travelers stop should cause you to recollect numerous other tourist-type places where coins are sure to await your metal detector:

Tourist stops of *any* any kind...wishing wells and bridges, hilltop lookouts, scenic spots.

Below all of the above or anywhere people might have pitched coins for luck.

Near litter cans on highways (but expect cans and pulltops).

Footpaths and resting spots along hiking trails or roadside parks.

And, Did You Think About?

Anywhere people congregate and anywhere people have been.

Around service stations, particularly older or abandoned ones.

Around old churches...where people might have gathered to visit after services...where they took "dinner on the grounds"...where children played.

Revival meeting sites.

Schools and colleges...around playground equipment, bicycle racks...in front of water fountains and doors, where students waited in lines.

Don't forget old or abandoned schools. In the East Texas area where I was reared is the old Steele Academy, a training school for boys that closed its doors before the turn of the century. This is good coin-hunting territory.

Where were the old schools and academies located in your area a century ago...150 years ago? How about the CCC camps and World War II training grounds of 50 years or so ago? Talk to old family members, friends and old-timers. Jog their memories about where people *used* to congregate.

Old highway cafes and truck stops...drive-in eating was a popular pastime throughout the United States for many years. Lots of coins were lost at such places.

Ghost towns...along the boardwalks...in the streets.

Around ladders and fire escapes permanently attached to buildings. As a boy, I recall playing on a slide-type fire escape from a church. I'm sure that I and others lost coins here.

Anywhere cars were parked...at sporting events... revivals...market areas.

Old stagecoach stops, relay points, trading posts.

Bus stops...school bus stops.

Around telephone booths.

Outdoor taverns...look for those with loose gravel.

Around flea markets and auctions.

Courthouses and other public buildings...around benches on the lawn, paths and walkways.

Are you beginning to understand that there is really no limit to the many types of locations where coins await your metal detector? Just think of the places where you have used coins...recall your own experiences. I'll bet you can come up with many locations that are not listed above.

Listen and Learn

There are oh-so-many people with whom you can talk to learn where coins and other valuables might have been lost or are being lost *right now*. Consider this list and, once again, add to it from your own background:

Old-timers of all kinds head the list. Let them talk about the past and the way things were "then."

Caretakers of parks and recreation centers.

Lifeguards at swimming areas. They can perhaps tell you about jewelry whose loss was reported.

Police and personal property insurance agents can also serve as sources of tips on lost valuables.

Highway clean-up crews know where people normally congregate...that's where they will lose coins.

Clergymen, especially older ones, can give you the locations where outdoor revival meetings were held in "the good old days."

Construction crews...especially those tearing down houses or buildings; as soon as they shut down for the night, try to be there with your detector...but, *obey* all safety rules and don't trespass.

THers have a personal sense of discovery when their impressive coin collections include coins they have found, such as the valuable gold piece at top

Historians, amateurs preferably, who can relate local history and point out where people once used to gather, transact business and play. A common occurrence is for the town sites to "wander;" that is, to move away from where the community was founded. Coins lost long ago won't "wander" until you dig them up!

History books are unbeatable sources of local information. Read *all* those written about your area. You'll learn from each of them. Don't assume that books have never been written about your area. Check with libraries and historical societies for manuscripts. Don't forget the chamber of commerce.

Research Is the Key

This entire subject of research is one that I can't stress enough. You may remember history from school as a jumble of dates and names, all dry as dust. When you're looking at a history of people who lost coins and valuables in places you can search, you'll find that it takes on a new and more attractive life. To me research can be as much fun as the actual treasure hunt. And, it's a part of this hobby that you can pursue any month of the year in any kind of weather.

Many people say, "I just don't have time for research," but this is the wrong attitude. The right kind of research *saves* you time and will greatly increase both quality and quantity of your finds. A good researcher will never find the time to follow through on all the great tips that he can discover.

I know because, unfortunately, I'm speaking from the experience of having more places to search than time to search them.

All THing can be a family affair, but this is especially true of coin hunting since even the youngest lad or lass appreciates the value of a shiny coin.

Visit museums and study old maps for locations of promising sites. Spend time at your library or newspaper reviewing the newspapers of yesteryear. Be particularly alert to the "lost and found" pages of yesterday as well as today.

Speaking of Newspapers

Make it a daily habit to read current newspapers with a special vigilance over the lost and found sections. Quite often people who lose valuables will advertise and post a reward for the return of these objects. When you see that a metal detector could find the valuable, contact that person who lost it and work out an agreement for your services. Perhaps the advertiser will pay you for your time or split the value of the article. You might search for it on your own.

Newspapers are filled with information on locations of public congregations (company picnics, family reunions). In reviewing the newspapers of yesteryear pay attention to learn the locations of old parks and playgrounds, band concert sites, fairground and circus lots and information on public activities that occurred in the past as well as notices of lost articles.

When reading newspapers, the true treasure hunter realizes that the only limit to success is the effort that is expended. Tresure-location possibilities abound!

This book is designed to stir your imagination...to help convince you that coins can be found everywhere, but I find it impossible to stress adequately the importance of research. It's truly the *key to success* in finding treasure with a metal detector. Certainly you are glad to pocket the "profits" of finding coins anywhere. You will discover, however, that the greatest personal rewards of this hobby as well as those of most monetary value come from finding valuable old coins through your own research, investigation and hard work. Even when you come home with pockets filled with coins, you may grow tired sometimes of digging up current coins in the parks and playgrounds. You'll never grow tired of recovering old, rare and valuable coins in places *you* discovered by your own desire and careful investigative efforts. You will only become more enthusiastic and your rewards will increase.

Take Me Along

If your metal detector could talk, it might sing this old Broadway song. And, if you're really interested in finding coins, you ought to listen!

You'd be amazed at the places where you can hunt coins just in your normal weekend and vacation traveling. For example, how about those old drive-in theaters you see along the roadsides? There aren't too many left, and the sites are fast filling up with houses and shopping centers. Still, there must be many coins in these fields with numismatic value equivalent to the cost of our finest metal detector. Deserted highway stops and cafes, roadside parks, camping, hunting and fishing parks can be found along many roads. Stops such as these can prove not only very profitable, but they also give you a chance to stretch your legs, walk the dog or make new friends for our hobby.

When you get off the Interstate Highways in your travels you pass through many towns and communities. Most of these have some kind of park, playground or swimming area. Drive to the parks and let your children play while you search the most likely places for rare coins. Don't forget to fill all holes you dig and to dispose of any trash you encounter or dig up. This may help calm that caretaker who wondered what you were doing digging up his park. Always visit historical markers. Many travelers stop here, rest, take pictures and lose coins. Who knows? You might dig up a treasure cache like the many which have been reported found around prominent historical and state border markers. At least you'll learn some more history!

Off the Beaten Path

When you have time in your travels, get off the main roads...especially if you're serious about coin hunting. The farther you can get from today's civilization the more likely you are to find old settlements and places where coin hunting is good. Why not check out the map before you leave on your next driving trip? Look for alternate routes. Take the back roads, and drive a little slower.

Obvious places may surprise you with the quantity of good old coins they yield. I'm talking about courthouses, parks, community recreation centers and such public places. You may be the first person ever to scan a metal detector over them. But, if you look for leads, you can do even better. Talk to people who are familiar with these little towns...people who can direct you to old campgrounds, settlers' meeting places, old fairgrounds and peddlers' stands. There are always some old timers sitting around the courthouse square or on the benches that remain on small town streets.

One approach is to go up to these senior citizens and ask, "Say, can you tell me where I can find an old timer in this town?" That generally brings a laugh and helps open them up. When they start talking about the past and where people gathered, you'll be amazed with the volume of information you can compile and how quickly you can gather it.

One story I like concerns an ethnic reunion that is still held annually in a Central Texas area. Literally hundreds of men, women and children would gather once a year in this particular location for a rousing picnic that was climaxed each year by considerable drinking of beer and wine and more than a few friendly brawls. Obviously, the location for this annual get-together is filled with coins...and the site is replenished annually. Yet, this is the type of information that can be found only through personal research with local citizens.

Did you make a wrong turn on that unmarked road? What's your hurry? Just drive along and see some new scenery until you return to your proper route. Stop and ask directions. Maybe you'll discover a new coin hunting location that you would never have found by taking the "right" road.

Picnic areas and roadside parks are favorite places for the traveling coin hunter. Search carefully around all tables and benches and out away from seating, especially in grassy areas. Look carefully around drinking fountains, along trails and around trees. Frequently, after eating, travelers will wander into grassy areas and lie down to rest. If areas are large, search places that are shady. Search where cars have been parked.

Churches and Brush Arbors

One of the oldest nickels I ever recovered was found five feet from the front doorstep of an old church. Five inches deep, it gave an excellent signal in our mineral-free East Texas soil. When searching around churches and tabernacles, look especially in front where people might have stood and talked after the services. They lost coins here. Also look around back and in trees where children might have played. Search areas where cars and buggies would have been parked. Old churches also usually had picnic areas which you should try to locate and search.

Never pass up the chance to search any area that was ever used as a "brush arbor" or site for outdoor revivals. A scattering of sawdust, long benches and an overhead brush covering provided an instant worship location. You can be certain that coins were lost here.

As an old friend liked to recollect, "Can't you just imagine some sleepy fellow sitting on the hard benches trying to stay awake and pay attention to a sermon. He gradually drifts off to sleep and, first thing he knows, someone is punching him in the ribs and waving a collection plate in his face. Of course, he's embarrassed and fumbles out some coins to drop in the plate. He *also* drops some coins in the sawdust that are still waiting there for us to find!"

On the Beach

No chapter on coin hunting would be complete without some discussion of searching for coins and other lost wealth on the beach. It's truly the new frontier for treasure hunting, and it's one that is rich with rewards. Any public beach, whether of an ocean, lake or river, is a good place to try your luck.

Sun worshipers and swimmers lose coins, rings, watches, medallions and all kinds of jewelry in almost unbelievable numbers. Why do people wear jewelry to the beach? Why don't they take better care of their money? Who knows? But, we treasure hunters can benefit! It's easy to understand how they lose things. Take rings, for instance. People go swimming, play

101

in the water or run and frolic on the beach in the heat. They perspire and douse themselves with suntan lotion. Rings quickly fall off slippery fingers and are quickly mashed into the sand. An individual generally has no idea where a ring was lost at the beach. The same is true for other jewelry... necklaces, watches and the like. Many people carry coins loose in an open pocket of a bathing suit or beach jacket. Such coins are just waiting to fall out and join the jewelry in the sand.

The best time to search a beach is immediately after the weekend or any time after crowds have been there. Make certain you arrive before the beach cleaners who sweep everything up when they rake the sand. If you'll spend some time with the people on the beach and watch where they play, you'll quickly determine the "hot spots" to search first...where the "bathing beauties" held court and where the "hot dogs" strutted their egos. Always look around concession stands, piers, lifeguard towers, drinking fountains and locations of that sort where people naturally congregate. Try working along the water's edge at both high and low tides. Both can be profitable. You will encounter less trash at the water's edge, but some very valuable coins and jewelry have been found far up on the beach where they might have been flung by high waves. They remain untouched and gradually sink deeper in the sand because they're away from beach traffic and beach cleaners.

A favorite tactic of mine is to begin searching a beach an hour or so before absolute low tide. I scan parallel to the water's edge and follow the tide out. You'll find much more on beach hunting in Chapter 12.

A word about equipment is mandatory in every discussion about the beach. Any of the new automatic detectors, such as those in Garrett's Ultra GTA or Freedom Plus Series, is satisfactory for the beach. Remember, however, that your detector must be protected from blowing sand, rain or splashing surf. The danger of water is obvious, but sand can be the real villain because it will seep through the tiniest crack in any detector...

Except for the environmentally protected models like Garrett's XL500 Sea Hunter. Not only is it protected against sand, but it is waterproof in case it's accidentally dunked or splashed. With circuitry especially designed to eliminate ocean-salt minerals, you can't beat the Sea Hunter for searching by the water. Underwater pulse induction detectors such as the Sea Hunter are also fine for the beach.

When hunting on the beach you should observe the same good manners that govern your coin hunting in the park or anywhere else. First and foremost...*fill your holes.*

Let me repeat that this chapter is designed to stir your imagination...to help convince you that coins can be found everywhere. I know that this is true, and so do millions of other hobbyists. Only by getting out in the field yourself — with a quality metal detector, preferably — can you appreciate the true excitement and the real joy of this hobby...excitement and joy, incidentally, that are substantially heightened by the *profit* motive!

9 – Finding the Big Money Treasures...

Cache Hunting

C ache hunting is *different*. Always remember that...no matter how successful you've been at finding coins...no matter how much jewelry you've dug out of the beach. Thus, this chapter has but one purpose: to help treasure hunters *find money!*

What? You may ask. Aren't all treasure hunting books designed to help me find money, one way or the other...coins in the park...jewelry at the beach...valuable relics in a ghost town? Yes, finding wealth of some type should be one of your goals whenever you go treasure hunting, along with other equally valuable goals...outdoor exercise and fresh air, the pleasure of relaxation and the thrill of discovery.

But this chapter is designed to explain how you must think and act *differently* when you hunt for a cache. Always remember you'll be looking for *big* (relatively speaking) *money*. True, you'll need all the knowledge you've developed in other kinds of hunting. And, your basic techniques may be the same as the ones you've always used. It's your overall manner of searching for a cache – from research to recovery – that must be quite different...if you are to be successful.

Looking for money caches generally means searching for a larger quantity of buried treasure. Your cache can be an iron kettle filled with gold or silver coins. It can be a cache of gold or silver bars or even guns. You will generally be looking for objects much larger than single coins...though smaller money caches in tobacco cans are sometimes found.

Before we discuss recovery techniques let's look for a moment at the true cache hunter – that "different" breed in our treasure hunting fraternity. This person is seldom seen among weekend hobbyists, those who hunt coins and relics just for the fun of it. The cache hunter spends his or her time in pursuit of larger, more profitable finds.

Yet, their reasons are not all financial. Nor, does the cache hunter consider hunting for coins or small relics to be beneath his or her dignity. It's just that searching for small objects never appealed to them; they seek "something big" just as the big game fisherman is willing to spend a lifetime in search of that record-breaking marlin or sailfish.

Metal detector techniques necessary for successful cache hunting differ somewhat from those used by coin hunters. In searching for coins, you generally used the Discriminate mode with occasional ventures into All Metal. For cache hunting, we suggest the opposite. In fact, to find caches most effectively, we recommend that you use the All Metal mode almost exclusively.

Let's say you're looking for an iron pot filled with coins. In such a situation your instrument would actually signal to you about the big pot...not all those coins inside it. If you were scanning with the Discriminate mode, the detector might reject the iron pot, and you'd never dig it. What a disaster! Use the All Metal mode, but remember what you've learned earlier and so many other times: If you seek *real* success, you must be prepared to dig lots of junk!

Does your cache hunting detector have a *true* non-motion All Metal mode? It better! The principal reason for using a non-motion All Metal mode can be spelled out in one word...depth. There's just no question that non-motion All Metal circuitry will probe deeper than any Discriminate mode. You can also achieve your own degree of ground balance since detectors with a genuine All Metal mode usually offer manual ground balance. If your cache is located in highly mineralized soil, you may need the precise ground balance offered by manual controls to be able to find it.

If you use a detector that offers only the Discriminate mode — even when you set it at zero — you want to be certain that your detector does not furnish any residual discrimination at this setting. Some detectors *will* supply you with some discrimination, even at a zero setting. Now, this little bit of discrimination may prevent nails and other small trash from being detected. But, it can prevent an iron container filled with coins from being detected as well.

All of Garrett's detectors are calibrated to offer *no* discrimination at the zero setting of their Discriminate mode. When using the instrument of another manufacturer, we urge that you test for yourself.

Unless you're searching for a cache in a building — where you know that it cannot possibly be too far away — always use the largest searchcoil possible. Remember that larger searchcoils can detect larger objects and detect them at greater depths. Money caches have been found at all depths (arm's length seems to be popular), but you want to be prepared for extremes. In some areas, where washing has occurred and drainage patterns have redesigned the landscape, caches have been found that were covered at different depths than when they were originally buried.

All the more reason to use the larger searchcoils — even the Depth Multiplier Bloodhound!

When searching a farmyard for a money cache, look closely at specific objects and obstacles in that yard, such as a well, the corners of the farmhouse and its chimney. Search inside the chimney and all outbuildings...especially those that contained animals.

Never fail to search an old garden area. Here's where the farmer's wife may have hidden some "rainy day" savings in a fruit jar. Remember that when people buried caches, they didn't want to be observed. It would be quite normal for a farm wife to hide a jar of money in her apron, carry it to some special location in the garden and "plant" it secretly.

When you are using the 12 1/2-inch searchcoil, and certainly the 8 1/2-inch size, these coils will detect objects far smaller than caches.

Therefore...expect some junk! When you suspect that the cache you are seeking is larger than a small fruit jar, we recommend that you use the Depth Multiplier, called the Bloodhound. This attachment multiplies by several times the depth detecting capability of any detector with which it is compatible. An important feature of the Depth Multiplier is that it will not detect small objects. In an old farmyard you can dig only larger and, possibly, more valuable targets because you won't ever be bothered by trash that is certain to be littering the soil.

It's easy to use the Depth Multiplier attachment with a compatible detector. Just get into the basic All Metal mode and forget about trying to adjust ground balance. Wear headphones and set your audio threshold for faint sound. Be sure you aren't carrying a large metal object such as a shovel or large knife even though a few coins in your pocket may not matter. Hold the detector and fully extend your arm. Let the detector cradle in your fingers. Slowly walk across the area you wish to search.

Listen carefully for an increase in the audio level. When you hear the louder sound, stop and scratch a mark on the ground with your shoe. Continue walking without adjusting any of the detector's controls. When you have walked across the object you have just detected, the audio will return to its threshold level. Walk a few more feet before turning around and walking a return path. At the point where the audio increases as you are walking from this direction, make another mark on the ground. Your target will lie at the center point between your two marks on the ground.

Bury A Cache

Successful searching for caches requires considerable experience...and thinking. You must learn to put yourself right in the shoes of the person who hid that cache for which you are searching. It's easy to understand why a person wouldn't just run out into his yard haphazardly and dig a hole to bury a jar full of gold coins. No, siree! If you were burying a cache, you'd select a secret place and a secret time to bury it...perhaps, at night during a thunderstorm. And, your "secret place" would be one that you could find in a hurry!

Practice this yourself. Put some money (or something similar) in a mason jar. Go outside your house and bury it. That's right. *Go ahead and bury it...*if only for a few minutes. After you've done this, you'll be able to ask yourself the questions that probably occurred to that person who hid any cache you ever seek.

Would you do it in broad daylight? Would you just walk out into the yard and start digging? Probably not, because you wouldn't want anyone to see what you were doing. So, choose the right time and the right place to bury your cache. Can I find it easily? Can it be found accidentally by a stranger? Will it be safe? Many other questions will come into your mind as you recover your own cache and relocate it a time or two. This is good experience that will make you a better cache hunter.

When you hear a story or get a treasure map about a cache that is buried high atop a mountain or in some other difficult-to-reach location, you'll ask yourself such questions as, "Why there?" Why, indeed would someone have climbed a high mountain or scaled a steep ravine to bury a cache?

You'll also learn that hard-packed soil is generally an indication that no cache is located beneath it. Most people are lazy. They would rather dig in softer soil or just bury a cache in a pile of loose rocks.

Try to learn the thinking of someone who is burying a cache, and you'll have better luck finding it. It won't be just "luck," either! Whenever you're tempted to attribute the success of another cache hunter to "luck," remember what the old football coach said when they accused his team of being lucky: "We had to be there for the luck to happen!"

Some of the most pleasant hours I've enjoyed in metal detecting have been spent with my good friend Roy Lagal in the beautiful Nez Perce country of northern Idaho searching for caches. In the summer of 1877 the Nez Perce Indians were suddenly uprooted and forced to leave their ancestral homeland. They necessarily left behind them many valuable things. Among these were numerous caches of coins and other treasures — some which they meant to recover later; others, which they simply "put down for keeps," which was a Nez Perce custom. Because they undertook their historic trek to Canada on such short notice, some of the caches were buried hastily. Incidentally, my novel, *The Missing Nez Perce Gold* presents in a fictional form the story of our search for the biggest of all their storehouses of hidden wealth.

Over the years Roy and I have hunted for these caches with various kinds of detectors. It is truly amazing how much more effective today's modern instruments are than those with which we were so well satisfied just a few years back.

The soil at most of these Rocky Mountain cache sites has a high content of mineralization, and the terrain is generally rugged. The first challenge for a detector, then, is to achieve precise ground balance that permits faint signals to be heard rather than background chatter. Secondly, searchcoils must be capable of operating at various heights above the ground because of rocks and other obstructions.

Another problem we encountered at the Nez Perce locations concerned "hot rocks," those geological *freaks* that cause even the finest modern detectors to signal metal falsely. Since modern detectors with discrimination enabled us to deal quite effectively with these little pests, we suggest that you employ such a detector in cache hunting — even though you'll be hunting almost exclusively in your All Metal mode. Additional problems may come with ground balancing, but your modern instrument can overcome this when handled properly. Plus, it is always good to have discrimination...especially when you need it.

Cache Hunting Basics

Because cache hunting is different, the basic concepts governing it are also somewhat different than those of other forms of treasure hunting. Following are the primary rules that have proven successful for most of us cache hunters:

— Hunt *only* with a cache hunting detector and the *largest* searchcoil available.

— Conduct *extensive* research; you can never know too much about your target and the individual(s) who hid it.

— Be *patient* throughout your effort, from planning to scanning to recovering...and even after you dig up your prize.

— Never *assume* that because your target may be big that it will be *easy* to find. Sure, some cache targets are quite large. But, they are generally deep as well and, thus, more difficult to locate.

Certainly, we do not suggest that you forget or ignore any of the techniques you have already developed in the use of your metal detector. By all means, remember to use all those special tricks that have proved so successful for you and your instrument! As I continue to emphasize in all of my books and articles, basic techniques of metal detecting remain the same because the laws of physics do not change. Rules for ground balancing and discrimination that were valid when you were hunting coins in the park will be just as accurate when you're seeking a cache in the mineralized soil of a deserted Rocky Mountain ghost town.

It's the manner in which you apply the basic techniques that determines whether you can be successful in cache hunting. Let's consider some factors that will govern your application of all basic techniques of treasure hunting. Each of these factors can enter into successful recovery of deeply buried caches:

— Geographic location of the treasure site;
— Ground condition of the site and vegetation covering it;
— Mineral content of the soil;
— Physical size of the cache (generally overestimated!);
— Depth of the cache;
— Changes that might have occurred at the site *since* the cache was buried (generally not considered!);
— Your detector and its searchcoil.

Misjudgment of any one of the above can keep you from recovering the prize you seek. Experienced cache hunters always make allowances for the condition of the search area and the fact that their cache may be both deeper and smaller than anticipated. Pay close attention to the description of where it was buried. And, when you reach the probable location of your cache, don't rule the site out just because of its present-day appearance. So what if it *doesn't* look like that description written decades or centuries ago! Remember that trees and shrubs grow taller or can die and be removed entirely. Plus, you should never underestimate the effects of both erosion and sedimentation. What was once a deep ditch might be just a depression today...and, vice versa.

Take your time. Be patient, and reap the rewards.

As you may already know from coin hunting experiences, the longer a coin has been buried, the easier it is to detect. Depending upon coil characteristics and other factors, freshly buried metallic objects can be detected to about one-half the depth of the same objects when buried for a longer time. This same phenomenon holds true in the detection of buried caches.

Searching Indoors

When searching for a money cache behind or inside a wall in a house, you can generally use either the All Metal or Discriminate mode. But, even when using the Discriminate mode, we recommend that you turn the discrimination controls to their lowest settings...just enough discrimination to eliminate nails from detection.

In either mode you'll have more than enough sensitivity to detect almost any size money cache in all walls, despite their thickness or type of construction.

When your treasure map leads you to a stucco wall containing a wire mesh, here are some tips to help you detect through that mesh. Place your searchcoil against the wall, set your detector in its Discriminate mode and lower discrimination control(s) to the minimum. By carefully sliding the searchcoil across the wall you can lessen interference from the mesh.

Seeking a deeply buried money box in the desert of the Texas-Mexico border, this THer equipped himself properly with research and equipment.

112

You may hear a jumbled mass of sound, but you should always listen for significant changes that could indicate you have located your cache.

Some prefer to search walls with a mesh by holding the searchcoil several inches or even a foot away from the wall. Getting the searchcoil this far away should take care of the jumbled sound, yet still let your detector detect large masses of metal such as a money cache.

What is a Cache?

Caches come in all sizes, and they're generally dreamed of as a Well Fargo money box, a big trunk or a set of saddle bags...all stuffed with gold coins, old bills, antique jewelry and the like. I sincerely hope that this describes the cache that you locate some day. In the meantime, please remember that most caches are small. They consist of a tobacco tin holding a few bills or a quart fruit jar filled with old coins. Not as exciting, perhaps, as the Wells Fargo box or those outlaw saddle bags, but valuable nonetheless.

Regardless of the size cache you seek, you must not take a chance. So, use a large searchcoil. There is no doubt that even the best treasure hunters have left deep caches that were beyond the range of the finest detectors available in earlier years. These caches await you and other hunters with the 21st-century instruments capable of finding them.

Perhaps it seems that this entire *Treasure Hunting Text* is "over-stressing" the importance of using a modern detector or one with the right size coil. Many failures in cache hunting, however, can be attributed to those hobbyists who are thoroughly familiar with the techniques of coin hunting but are inexperienced in seeking the deeper and larger prizes. Because they have full confidence in their detectors to locate

The properly attired cache hunter wears headphones, uses a Bloodhould depth multiplier and carries a long-handled shovel to dig up his discovery.

deep coins, they may overestimate their abilities to hunt for caches. Since the cache is large, they believe they have all the capabilities needed to locate it.

So, they envision themselves as cache hunters and conduct proper research to develop a good lead at, say, an old church or mission site. It was used as a hideout after a robbery, and the loot — believed to have been buried there — has never been recovered. A great deal of time is obviously required by this research, and reaching the site may call for considerably more time, plus expenses that can include the purchase of additional equipment.

Finally, after this expenditure of time, money and emotional energy, the "wannabe" cache hunters are on site...ready to scan for the long-lost payroll, or whatever. Only, the scanning is done with a coin-hunting detector with automatic ground balance, a Discriminate mode and an 8-inch searchcoil. If the area contains mineralized soil (and, this always seems to be true) the instrument must be able to penetrate this mineralization with ground balance capable of compensating for it. The coin hunting detector will leave our wannabe cache hunters almost helpless...and they won't even know it!. Perhaps they will be able to salvage something from the trip by locating a relic or two — maybe, even an old coin!

Occasionally, you can actually see the above scenario portrayed in treasure magazines. The article is all about an alleged "cache hunting" expedition and is accompanied by a photo of the hunters on-site. Look at their searchcoils. If they are small, this hunt may have produced a few relics but probably not a cache...certainly not one that was buried deeply in mineralized soil.

Imagine scanning *right over* a valuable cache simply because your detector did not have the power or the sensitivity to detect it. Of course, that's exactly what happened to so many of the talented old-timers who used early-day detectors. They didn't even know when they were scanning over the caches that still are waiting today for our modern 21st-century instruments!

Research

Most cache hunters spend a major portion of their time in research, seldom mentioning their occupation except to another professional. Since proper research can require extensive travel, expenses necessary simply to determine the *existence* of a single cache can be considerable even before a detector is assembled and turned on. Sometimes, cache hunters are required to pay sizable sums to obtain information. Often, they agree to share the cache on a percentage basis, a common practice also for gaining permission to search on private property. Occasionally, a special detector must be purchased because of the nature of the ground where a cache is sought. Proper financing, as well as patience, is required.

The cache hunter is willing to overcome all these obstacles because he or she is seeking real treasure — financial wealth — and a bundle of it! In fact, dedicated cache hunters perversely welcome the obstacles since they limit the number of hobbyists in the field searching for the same prizes. Successful cache hunters are a dedicated breed, but their single-mindedness pays off in tangible rewards.

Of course, not all are successful every time. The beginner should realize this and not become discouraged. We advise working on several projects simultaneously. Since research can be so expensive, it is good to "double-up" on the uses you can make of it. Always remember that there are literally millions of dollars stashed in the ground waiting to be found. If you persist, sooner or later you will hit a cache. It may be only a few hundred dollars tucked in a tobacco tin; then again, some treasure hunters have become wealthy from pursuing this fascinating occupation.

Never pass a suspected treasure site because you have been told that it has been worked before. You don't know who searched or when or with what kind of detector! Also, I'm convinced that no matter how often a site may have been searched over the years, more treasures were missed than were recovered. In researching my novel *The Secret of John Murrell's Vault*, my editor Hal Dawson and I returned to a location where – just like Gar Starrett – I once found only a deep and empty hole instead of the treasure I expected. As we reinspected this hole, it occurred to us that maybe the *real* treasure had been buried even deeper, with only a sampling of items left in a container above to satisfy anyone who might accidentally stumble upon this site!

Concerning "worked-over" sites, just consider the old parks where coins continue to be found year after year after year...and, not all of them newly minted coins either. These parks never seem to be completely hunted out. Now, consider the rugged, highly mineralized terrain where many caches are found and consider also the eternal question of just how deeply they were actually buried. These caches are far harder to find than coins. Remember, also, that anyone who searched a site in past years probably did so with a detector whose capabilities are far exceeded by your newer, modern instrument.

Never forget that modern detectors give you a tremendous advantage over the "old pros." I sincerely believe that even a relatively inexperienced treasure hunter with a detector from our new CX family of computerized instruments can search an area more effectively than the most experienced veteran cache hunter who insists on using an obsolete BFO or TR detector.

New computerized detectors such as my Grand Master Hunters CX II and III and the Master Hunter CX (the only computerized instruments with true non-motion All Metal modes...at this writing) will search deeper and with more precise ground balance. I urge that you give them a chance to help you find the big money prizes that have long been waiting for cache hunters. The opportunities have never been better! No matter how much skill an old timer had, he could not possess the *scientific abilities* of our modern metal detectors.

Use the new Grand Master Hunter CX III, multiply its depth capability with a Bloodhound searchcoil and discover a cache that *others* left behind.

Recovery Tools

Since most THers don't get involved with a cache that requires a bulldozer or backhoe, a long-handled shovel is the primary recovery tool. I also recommend a long steel probe that you can use to save time...where soil conditions permit. If you believe that your detector's response indicates a target large and deep enough to conform to the cache for which you are searching, you can probe the spot before digging. Length of your probe will determine how deep you can search. Experienced operators recommend one at least 40 inches long. They have learned to probe carefully to establish just what kind of target they have discovered. Of course, before you even stick a probe in the ground, you already have a good idea of what you are looking for. *That helps!*

You'll know easily if your probe hits a glass or a piece of junk metal it can easily penetrate. If you find a tin can, the probe may penetrate it to let you know if something is inside. Depth at which the object is found can give you some idea when it was buried. Many cache hunters who use probes become so proficient with them that they can feel a newspaper when the probe passes through it. The real old-timers even claim to be able to *read* the newspaper with their probe!

I recommend that you build your own special probe that has a steel ball bearing actually welded at the point of the shaft. A 1/2-inch bearing welded onto a 3/8-inch steel rod permits your probe to move up and down easily with no restrictions and lets you find out more easily just what you may have found.

Low Profile

Most experienced cache hunters go to great lengths to avoid calling attention to themselves. One way to do this is to carry detectors and all other equipment into the field in a backpack. You then appear to be just another hiker. A large backpack will usually accommodate a 12-inch searchcoil as well as a Depth Multiplier attachment, along with small shovels, your detector's housing and the other tools necessary for an average recovery.

There are numerous reasons for not calling attention to yourself or your search for caches. First of all, you're looking for money; 'nuff said. Plus, you'll be busy and won't need the attention of even honest curiosity-seekers. And, if word ever gets out about your recovery of a cache, you'll be amazed at the number of people who will try to take it away from you...legally by claiming rights to all or a part of it...or, simply, by force.

Never put your trust in a *verbal* agreement. A wise man once said that verbal agreements aren't worth the paper they're written on. Also, never leave an open hole after you have discovered something. Even a landowner with whom you have an agreement can get excited about a large hole. He visualizes it filled with gold coins, and trouble may lie ahead.

When you are working with partners, make certain that all arrangements are made in writing *before* you start spending money on research and equipment and, certainly, before any cache is discovered. Many of us have had unpleasant experiences, particularly in working with inexperienced treasure hunters, such as landowners. Generally, you can trust an experienced cache hunter who can't afford to have his reputation clouded by a squabble over property rights. Plus, he has handled "found money" before and doesn't tend to get as excited about it.

It's the novice you need be concerned about. Perhaps he simply supplied the tip that began a long and arduous search. Once the prize is recovered, you'll be amazed at how possessive this person can get about "my" treasure. Why, you may even be offered a "little something" for your time and effort in "helping find it!" Don't ever let this happen to you. Get everything in *writing* before you search.

Taxes must also be a subject of concern for any successful cache hunter. The Federal Government demands its percentage of income you derive from treasure hunting just like that from an investment or salary. Similarly, states and municipalities that tax income aren't satisfied until they get their proportionate share.

120

Yet, who'll know just what you actually recovered out there in the wilderness, much less its eventual worth? That's a good question. Always remember, however, that evading taxes is a crime punishable both by fine and imprisonment. In addition, rewards are given to any individual whose tip leads to the discovery of tax evasion. It's always been my advice, therefore, to pay all taxes that are due and to pay them when they are due. If you can prove that you're in the treasure hunting business, proper expenses can be deducted. Requirements differ from state to state. So, study them carefully; but never pay a cent more than you owe!

Again, my advice to a cache hunter is to keep a low profile in every way. Don't call attention to yourself. Pay your legitimate taxes. Insist on your rights...in a quiet, yet firm, manner.

If you haven't experienced the thrill of cache hunting, you can't know what you've missed. True, you'll experience the same thrill of discovery and the benefits of relaxation, fresh air and outdoor exercise that you get from other forms of treasure hunting. But, you'll give yourself the exciting chance of making that *really big* discovery...the thrill that should come to everyone at least once in a lifetime!

Relic Hunting

Searching battlefield and other areas for lost relics is not considerably different from cache hunting. Perhaps one difference is that the targets you are seeking are usually quite smaller, such as a single button or spent projectile. Techniques of scanning and locating, however, remain the same.

In the literal sense of the word "battlefield relics" are scarce indeed in the United States. Since the Civil War of 1861-65, our great nation has been blessedly free of wars fought on its soil. Even before then, the only actual war "battles" fought in what is now the United States were those in the East Coast states during the American Revolution and the War of 1812 and a skirmish or two in Texas during the Mexican War.

But, "war battlefields" notwithstanding, there are relics aplenty to be found. The richest trove of all, of course, is located in the Southern states where so many Civil War battles occurred. Fights with Indians left vast quantities of relics to be found throughout what was once frontier country. In addition to these obvious "battles" were many other skirmishes and actions of arms that resulted in relics to be found by today's metal detectors.

And, the term "relics" includes far more than implements of war and destruction. In fact, the dictionary definition is "a trace of the past." Collections specialize in relics from almost every sector of society and life. For example, when you're searching "out West," don't neglect antique barbed wire that is found by your detector. Just a single strand of old fencing can give you a real history lesson when you research it. And, it can be valuable to a collector as well.

What size searchcoil should you use when hunting for relics? You may be thinking that if you seek a small bullet, you shouldn't use the large 12 1/2-inch searchcoil. Wrong! The large searchcoil will detect almost any tiny projectile, button or coin that you might find on an old battlefield. Because you will need all the depth possible when searching battlefields, especially when the battles were fought years ago, we urge you to use the larger searchcoil. If, even with a light and easy-to-handle detector, you find this large coil too heavy for a full day's scanning, use an arm rest. This accessory provides counter-balance for the detector and enables you to use your instrument with less muscle fatigue.

Because so many battle sites are in low-lying or swampy areas, it is well to make certain that your searchcoil is submersible. Don't be confused by such designations as "splashproof" or "waterproof." You will want a searchcoil that can be completely submerged two feet or so...to the cable connector that attaches to the control housing. If in doubt about your searchcoil's capabilities, ask your dealer or manufacturer. All Garrett Crossfire searchcoils, of course, are submersible.

You perceptive treasure hunters already know what comes next, but I'll repeat, anyway: For maximum depth and sensitivity, use headphones and set your audio controls for the faintest threshold you can hear. This advice has been proven worthwhile over the years.

As worthwhile as the following advice...scan slowly. Your goal will be to cover an area methodically, completely and thoroughly. Grid search an area if you can by tying lengths of ropes to create grid squares and carefully searching each square before moving on to the next.

We recommend that you operate in the non-motion All Metal mode for greatest depth. Precise ground balancing circuitry on modern detectors, such as *Fast Track* on all of Garrett's CX detectors will solve your mineralization problems. Of course, large amounts of trash in the ground may cause you to readjust detector controls. If you're really not concerned about losing just an occasional target, operate in the Discriminate mode — but, with only a slight amount of discrimination. You'll miss small iron objects (including trash!), but will detect other objects such as lead, brass, bronze and, of course, coins to great depth.

Now, most experienced relic hunters would be aghast at reading that last statement. They use absolutely *no* discrimination. Here's one reason why: If a valuable coin is lying right next to an iron object and you are using discrimination, the iron object may cancel out the coin, causing you to miss it.

In relic hunting and battlefield searching, it is of the utmost importance that your detector be precisely ground balanced. As you have learned, *Fast Track* circuitry makes this an easy matter with Garrett's CX detectors. Even when extreme mineralization causes an excessive amount of audio change, you can use the manual controls to ground balance the instrument as precisely as you wish. When you do this, you'll know that signals you receive from your detector come from targets and not from ground mineralization.

When they are properly ground balanced to compensate for minerals present in the soil modern metal detectors can be operated with the searchcoil scanning at a height of up to four or more inches. The depth capabilities of these instruments permits the searchcoil to be held this high when necessary to clear weeds and brush as well as such objects as stumps and rocks. Of course, for best results the searchcoil should always be held as close to the ground (and the targets below it) as possible.

Another seemingly obvious tip is to double-check your hole always...no matter what kind of target you uncover. Of course, you should always double check every hole no matter what kind of hunting you are engaged in. If, for example, you're seeking large objects with the Depth Multiplier, always check your holes with a smaller searchcoil (or Garrett's Pocket Probe) to make certain that no smaller valuables are hiding in them...or that some other target isn't buried just an inch or two deeper. Just because you've dug up one relic doesn't mean that there can't be another in the exact spot! In fact, more likely than not, battlefield relics *should* be discovered in "clusters." They were probably lost that way!

Because any battlefield might contain explosives, take all necessary precautions. Any time you dig into an object and you suspect it might be an explosive, consult an authority...quickly! Remember that many guns are lost while still loaded and that even old ammunition that has been in the ground a number of years can still be fired. Don't get into arguments with explosives of any kind. It might prove dangerous to your health!

A military historian recently told me the story of how he owed his life to a Garrett detector. While scanning in Korea, he often found remains of Chinese soldiers still bearing live hand grenades. The advance warning provided by his Garrett permitted him to call in a bomb squad to dispose of the explosives.

The same need for precaution holds true for underground power cables. If you're detecting to great depths with the Bloodhound, you might occasionally find an underground cable.

Stop digging immediately! Contact the appropriate authorities, and inform them fully so that they can inspect your site and cover it properly.

Research

How to locate areas where you can search for relics? Your answer, again, is research...research and more research. Often times, all the research in the world cannot answer the question of exactly battle action occurred in a particular area or whether gunfire took place at that precise location. Only your detector can prove the locations of battle or gunfire by locating cartridges, bullets or other spent projectiles.

Research is particularly important since so many of the "obvious" locations to search for relics are now located in various state and national monuments and parks where the use of metal detectors is either banned entirely or highly restricted. You'll need to seek out locations about which only you and few others know...perhaps you can develop these by learning more about the history of your ancestors.

Indeed, metal detectors can help you rewrite history. This was proved by the extensive survey taken at the Custer battlesite at the Little Big Horn River in Montana. Study of the relics found by metal detectors helped increase the knowledge of where troopers and Indians died, but, more importantly, also changed perceptions of how they died. Evidence proved that Army weapons captured by Indians during the battle were turned on Custer's Cavalrymen in the final frenzy of the massacre.

Why Search for Relics?

Unlike the cache hunter, who is searching primarily for monetary reward, there are other reasons to search for relics and battlefield souvenirs. Some relic hunters are always looking for evidence to prove history, while others seek significant objects to add to a personal collection. Of course, many relics are sold, some for surprisingly large sums, and most relic hunters search for all of the above reasons.

It is fascinating to read tales of the early day settlers of this nation who simply picked up relics while plowing cropland or discovered them under brush in old battlefields. Those days have passed long ago. Except for those washed up or un-covered by storms, most of the visible relics have probably been found. Those remaining are below the earth's sur-face...sometimes far below...and can be located only by the modern ground-balanced metal detector.

Just as we advised you to find battlefield sites through research, research, research...we now urge that you practice, practice, practice to understand all that there is to know your metal detector and the way it reports its findings. Read the Owner's Manual for your detector so often that you can almost commit it to memory. Write or call the manufacturer if you have additional questions. Learn what to expect from your metal detector so that you will know what it is telling you in the field. Remember that your metal detector will always signal you about exactly its circuitry can find lying beneath the searchcoil. These signals, of course, are based on the quality of the detector's circuitry but are regulated by ground balance and/or discrimination controls designed by its manufacturer and adjusted by you. *Your metal detector will never lie to you!* But, you must interpret the truths that it reveals.

Of course, you'll want to cover all holes properly, no matter where you hunt. This is true whether you're on prominent display with your detector and digging tools or whether you're searching in a secret location only you know about. In public you're the example of our hobby, and we always want our "best foot forward." Out in the boondocks you don't want to leave any evidence that could lead other relic hunters to your secret spot. You *know* you haven't found everything that is there!

Ghost Towning

G host towns are veritable wonderlands for a treasure hunter! Searching them encompasses all phases of the hobby. Looking for caches, seeking coins, hunting for relics...all of these can be pursued enjoyably in a ghost town, as well as the search of buildings, cabins and other structures that were once occupied.

Hunting in and around ghost towns...ghost towning, we call it...is quite similar to general THing. When searching ghost towns, you may one day be hunting in an area that contains only a few relics. Then, the next day, you might encounter an entire town; that is, structures still intact with buildings and rooms in them just as they were when people — for some reason — left, perhaps decades ago.

Any place where people once lived or conducted business will produce treasure that can be located by a metal detector. Thousands of abandoned homesteads, stores and commercial establishments, schools and churches as well as townsites, forts and military installations await you. The list of places where people "used-to-be-but-no-longer-are" is truly endless.

And, many of these locations have never been searched! We have discussed more than once the importance of not being intimidated by the fact that a specific location has been searched before. Remember that metal detector capabilities have improved dramatically in just the past few years and that the proficiency of individuals can vary widely...even with the best and most modern instruments.

To search ghost towns properly you must learn the techniques of hunting outdoors. But, you must also learn how to hunt in structures of all kinds. Never forget that incredible treasure caches have been located in the walls, floors and ceilings of old buildings.

When you're searching a building with a metal detector, also keep in mind that most wooden structures contain a truly countless number of nails.

You can expect your detector to respond with multiple target signals. Of course, you don't want to tear into a wall just to locate a nail. We recommend, therefore, that you search in the Discriminate mode, using only enough discrimination dialed in to reject troublesome small nails.

You'll not be likely to overlook a large money cache!

When scanning around window and door frames, be alert for signals you receive from the iron sashes used to suspend the window frames. Don't rip open a wall looking for treasure until you have exhausted all techniques for peering into that wall by other means. Most wall areas can be visually inspected simply by pulling slightly back on a single board and shining a flashlight into the cavity. Never tear down or otherwise destroy old buildings. In fact, you should let all structures remain just as you found them...without harm or defacement of any kind. Walk away leaving all ghost town sites in such condition that no one can really tell whether you found treasure there or not.

Brick chimneys are familiar occurrences in many abandoned buildings, and treasures have been found behind their loose bricks. Remember, however, that most bricks are made of highly mineralized clay with iron in the conductive soil from which they were baked. Is this an impossible problem? Not for a modern metal detector with circuitry that lets you ground balance it precisely! Simply ground balance your detector against a chimney just as you would against the ground. Most likely you'll find no chimney stones or bricks that you cannot

Author uses modern detector to inspect carefully the ruins of this ghost town for any type of valuable or cache that might have been hidden in a wall.

properly ground balance. Be alert, of course, to nearby metal or to pipes within the chimney. You cannot ground balance your detector if metal is present.

Ghost towns will present detector hobbyists with a seemingly endless amount of junk iron of all shapes and sizes. If you are looking for coins, brass objects or other similar targets, therefore, use the Discriminate mode with only a small amount of discrimination. It would take weeks or months — perhaps, even years — to dig every metal target to be found in a ghost town. This makes discrimination mandatory. But, let me urge that you employ all techniques we have already considered...the smaller Super Sniper searchcoil, minimum discrimination, slow scanning, careful study of questionable targets, etc.

When looking for money caches, use a larger searchcoil or the Depth Multiplier. All ghost towns had a trash dump, and these sources of potential prizes can be located quite easily through methodical use of a Depth Multiplier.

Because of all the junk you are certain to find you must develop techniques for properly identifying targets before you dig. Rely heavily on your detector's meter or visual target display to do this for you. And, try to learn more about how your detector identifies targets both audibly and visually. Especially when searching ghost towns should you pay close attention to both audio and ID meter or graphic readout signals. Try to correlate the audible and visual signals before making a decision on digging a specific target.

If available on your detector, the Belltone mode of sound will be helpful here because most iron objects will then simply increase your sound level while objects of conductive metal such as coins and objects of brass and bronze will respond with the distinctive Belltone.

The old Western U.S. Cavalry post, above, is an ideal place to search for all types of treasure, such as relics, gold nuggets or the cache of coins at bottom.

Simply hearing a signal will often let you know in which range your target falls. Always inspect the LCD display or meter to see if it agrees with the audio, which will usually be the case. There will be times, however, when only a faint blip might cause you to suspect a target should be rejected, yet your display indicates it to be made of metal with high conductivity. Dig to determine if the target is junk such as a large stove lid (which might be a relic itself!) or something that has simply overridden the electromagnetic field of the searchcoil.

In areas with lots of junk targets your audio may sound often with blips and other sharp signals as well as an occasional coin tone. If using one of the new computerized instruments, remember that your detector is hunting deeper than other detectors. Consequently, it will give you more signals over a given spot of ground than another instrument that is not detecting as deeply. You have several options that will cut down on these sounds. First, you can reduce detection depth to 50% or below and still probably have sufficient depth for most targets in a ghost town. Also, you can reduce threshold almost to silent to reduce spurious signals. Try various combinations of adjustments such as these to achieve optimum audio for any difficult ground you encounter.

What about searching houses where people still live? Provided they are old enough and have enough "history," occupied homes can present many targets. You can look for caches hidden and forgotten by previous dwellers. You can seek jewelry or silverware that was hidden for safekeeping and never recovered for some reason. You can find coins and other items of value that might have fallen through cracks to rest under floorboards or between walls.

Truly, treasure waits to be found wherever men and women have been. Humans misplace, lose and hide items of value in locations where they can be discovered only by a modern metal detector. Of course, never fail to use your eyesight in searching any location. What can be discovered simply lying on the ground or on the floor of a structure is amazing.

When you are searching an old cabin or house or hunting anywhere else in a ghost town, however, you should understand that surface items were probably picked up by relic and antique hunters long, long ago. You will need a quality metal detector because most of the objects you seek are lying beneath the ground or are concealed from sight in some other way.

When someone tries to dissuade you from hunting anywhere by telling you that an area has already been searched, we suggest that you answer, "I've never searched it myself with *this* metal detector." Perhaps you will find something that was overlooked previously because either the detector or its operator did not have the capabilities of you and your instrument. Perhaps it will be something very valuable!

Since research is first on the "to-do" list of any competent treasure hunter, you will want to find out specifically where to find ghost towns or buildings and cabins that can be searched. There are many books on this subject that can be studied at your local library or at the shop of your metal detector dealer. Historical societies and tourist bureaus are excellent sources for this information. Ghost town maps are sometimes available.

A Family Pastime

Searching old buildings and cabins in a ghost town is a pastime that you can combine with a family vacation. Perhaps your travels take you to unusual and interesting places...old abandoned towns and mining areas. Can you believe that thousands of tourists travel through such areas without stopping? Yes, even metal detector hobbyists who don't realize all that they are missing! Relics, old coins and other valuable items are just waiting to be found. In many of the areas that especially cater to tourists, you will find libraries and visitor facilities especially equipped to suggest places for you to search with a metal detector. These free sources of information are generally more accurate than hand-drawn maps and guides you receive from individuals.

Don't forget all the many things that you have learned about research, however! Use these techniques to the fullest. Remember how helpful old-timers can be and what you can learn from long- time residents. In many of the tourist areas, unfortunately, you will discover that local citizens are not particularly interested in strangers, especially if the strangers are not important to their livelihood. Some hobbyists become discouraged when they receive little or no information from local citizens or are treated almost rudely. Don't you give up! Good people exist, and there is always the library. Keep looking for "that spot" where you can find treasure with your metal detector. Persevere, and you will be successful.

Discrimination

Modern metal detectors are ideally suited for searching cabins and buildings, even those with thousands upon thousands of small nails. These small, iron objects made searching houses oh-so-difficult for many of the older detectors. You'll still encounter some problems, but the modern detector with precise discrimination permits you to search buildings quite easily. And, you can be certain that you've searched thoroughly!

Because your main goal will be to detect small, coin-sized objects, your standard searchcoil approximately eight inches in diameter is a good choice. The smaller Super Sniper coil may be an even better choice. Because it is smaller, you can get it into tighter places. Too, with its narrower diameter the Super Sniper won't be reporting about as many nails in its electromagnetic field.

A cache that is still intact in an abandoned building will generally be some type of ferrous or metal container. We used to recommend that no discrimination be used in searching for such a prize, but the new detectors with precise controls have outmoded this advise. As indicated above, use just enough discrimination to get you past the nails. Even the cache in a small tobacco tin should generate a signal that you can hear.

Some treasure hunters use a little more discrimination, especially when searching around the large nails present in joists and rafters. Use one of these large nails for bench testing and increase the discrimination control of your detector until the nail is ignored. At this level of discrimination, set your audio threshold just above the silent level with only a faint sound and search with the searchcoil approximately four inches or so away from the walls and ceilings. Your audio response should remain fairly even and enable you to locate all ferrous objects larger than the nail for which you have set your discrimination. If the sound is still too erratic or jumpy, decrease the sensitivity (depth) control for easier operation.

Too much discrimination could cause the detector to reject a tobacco tin, small can or iron box. Too little discrimination permits the detector to respond so loudly to small nails that you might miss larger valuable objects. Regardless of your discrimination level, a modern detector will respond to non-ferrous targets as small as a coin. Practice in your own home with various levels of discrimination.

Non-Ferrous Targets

When you're searching for such non-ferrous targets as a coin cache in a glass jar or earthen pot, different procedures are needed. You will want to use both the All-Metal as well as the Discriminate mode of your detector. Essentially, you will be searching in the All Metal mode and switching to Discriminate to check out targets you encounter.

After setting your audio threshold, adjust your discrimination controls to reject large ferrous targets such as iron pipes, tin cans and large nails. Begin searching in the All Metal mode. When you have located a target, pinpoint it and move your searchcoil away slightly. Then, switch to the Discriminate mode and press the searchcoil against the wall directly over your suspected target.

When the target consists of coins, brass or some non-ferrous object, the sound will remain positive. Practice by locating a known iron target such as a window sash inside a wall. Place a non-ferrous target such as a piece of brass, aluminum or bag of coins nearby. First, pinpoint the good target in your All Metal mode. Switch to Discriminate, and the detector will respond positive even though it is only inches away from the large piece of iron.

Always make certain to let the searchcoil remain in contact with the wall surface when attempting to identify all targets.

When you slide the searchcoil over a wall to pinpoint targets, the searchcoil will sometimes come very close to or in direct contact with a nail. You will hear a small, sharp response, which you soon should be able to identify. Either ignore this response or pull your searchcoil back several inches and double check.

Sensitivity

Many of the early detector models, even with discrimination, could not be operated effectively among metallic targets such as these small building nails. Retuning was a continual problem. Modern instruments have eliminated this problem, even while increasing sensitivity. In the old days, as detectors began to improve we appreciated the sensitivity of the early VLF models, but we had to grit our teeth while getting metallic responses. Sometimes, we'd say, "Well, you can turn a sensitive detector down, but you can't turn up one that's not sensitive at all!"

Now, we can have our cake and eat it too; that is, have ultra sensitivity, along with discrimination that lets us detect most effectively with it!

You'll be surprised at how many old buildings and cabins you can find to search. Just a few points to remember: Never tear down or otherwise destroy old buildings. In fact, you should leave all structures in better condition than you found them...without harm or defacement of any kind. Walk away from buildings and cabins that you have searched, leaving them in such condition that no one can really tell whether you found treasure there or not. Destroy nothing. Do not tear out any boards that you cannot replace easily. Use common courtesy at all times. Remember, you might want to return!

Do your research homework to locate lost and forgotten ghost towns. Find them, and then search thoroughly. It will pay financial dividends as well as enable you to relive history.

12 – Finding Lost Coins, Rings, Jewelry...

Beach Hunting

There's wealth to be found near the water! Over two thirds of the earth's total surface — nearly 200 million square miles — is water. Since the dawn of mankind, man has lived on or near water. Commerce, recreation, exploration, warfare and the search for food have compelled men and women to return to water every time they have strayed. And, whenever man made contact with water, he generally brought along valuable items, some of which were inevitably lost.

The world's oceans, lakes and streams, therefore, offer vast storehouses of lost wealth that await the treasure hunter. Beaches at the entrance to Davy Jones locker present the most accessible areas for hobbyists to begin searching. Beaches are attractive to the metal detector hobbyist for still another reason. As rules and regulations for using detectors increase in complexity, public beaches and the waters they touch grow even more appealing as a recreational location...as a site for pursuing our hobby.

And, new modern metal detectors make finding seaside wealth as simple as locating pennies lost in a park. At the water's edge, however, you'll be looking for expensive jewelry or relics from shipwrecks with today's detectors. These marvelous instruments are designed to overcome both the mineralization of beach sands (terrific in some areas) and the effect of wetted salt (always bad) in ocean water. There was no way — even just a few years ago — that the most modern detectors could have been used under such conditions. Yes, today's detectors have truly opened a new frontier. Come and explore it!

My advice to any THer is to become a beachcomber. The joys are countless, and the rewards are constantly surprising! Just what is a beachcomber? I describe him or her simply as a person who searches along shorelines. And, what are they seeking? Just about everything! There's always plenty of flotsam, jetsam and other refuse. Often, it's merely junk, but it can be lost wealth.

Wherever people congregate (or, have congregated), treasure can be found. Beach treasures awaiting the THer include coins, rings, watches, necklaces, chains, bracelets and anklets, religious medallions and crucifixes, toys, knives, cigarette cases and lighters, sunshades, keys, relics, bottles, fishnet balls, ships' cargo and other items that will soon fill huge containers. Out of sight below the sand lies that blanket of treasure awaiting the metal detector. Always remember, however, that the value of any treasure is ultimately determined only by its finder. Keeper finds can be anything from a weathered float to a costly piece of jewelry. And, for some lucky, persistent and talented hunters, their dream will come true. They will indeed find that chest of treasure hidden by some buccaneer or 17th-century Spaniard or Frenchman who never returned to claim his cache.

Oftentimes, the greatest joy for the beachcomber comes simply from walking the beach, from experiencing soft winds off the water and feeling the sand under bare feet while listening to the tranquilizing sounds of surf and seabreeze. The rewards of THing are but an added bonus.

It's hard to understand why people wear jewelry to the beach. Yet, they do, and they often forget...even about valuable heirlooms and diamond rings. But, whether sun bathers and swimmers care about their possessions or not, it's the same for the beachcomber. All rings expand in the heat; everyone's fingers wrinkle and shrivel, and suntan oils hasten the inevitable losses. Beachgoers play ball, throw frisbees and engage in horseplay. This flings rings from fingers and causes clasps on necklaces, bracelets and chains to break. Into the sand drop valuables where they quickly sink out of sight.

When you walk out onto a beach, where do you begin? How do you select the most productive areas? This is possibly the question I am asked most frequently by beginning beach hunters (and, more experienced ones as well). The answer, first of all, is that nobody should go pell-mell onto a beach and begin hunting here and there without a plan. This is truly for beginners. To find treasure you must begin by being at the right place at the right time with the right equipment. Research sources will indicate the right place. Discussions of weather, tides and beach selection elsewhere in this chapter will often rescue someone studying a new beach.

The dedicated THer always first answers the question of "Where?" with research. Beyond that, experience must be the teacher. Inquiring and attentive hobbyists continually pick up ideas from other more veteran beachcombers, but the final decisions must be based on individual perceptions and intuition. Experience alone will educate the beach hunter about places that never produce and other places that are often rewarding.

Never overlook the possibility of finding flotsam and jetsam washing ashore from offshore shipwrecks. Regardless of the age of a wreck, some cargo — especially gold, silver, copper and bronze objects — will probably remain in fair to excellent condition for years, decades or even centuries. Gulf Coast and Caribbean shipwreck locations still yield silver and gold from the mines of Mexico and Peru. Gold and silver from California and other western states can be found along the Pacific coast.

Stay alert to current weather conditions. You'll want to search at low tides — the lower the better. After storms come ashore, head for the beach. When oil spills deposit tar and oil on beaches, there's a good possibility bulldozer and other equipment used to remove it can get you much closer to treasure. Watch for beach development work. When pipelines are being laid and when seawalls, breakwaters and piers are being constructed, work these areas of excavation.

You must develop the skill needed to "read" a site. If you learn which features are important and which are not, much of your battle is already won. As you research records, histories and old maps, be on the alert for clues to landmarks and locations. For instance, the name of a beach led me to a valuable Spanish icon that is very precious to me. Wouldn't a name like "Massacre Beach" cause your ears to perk up? Let me tell you of this experience where visual and mental study led me almost directly to one of those "X-marks-the-spot" locations.

Submerged at the entrance to a cove on the beautiful Caribbean island of Guadaloupe were numerous old and very large anchors protruding a few feet out of the water. Quite an unusual sight! The anchors had been placed there centuries ago to prevent enemy ships from entering the cove which then served as a harbor. It took little imagination to visualize enemy ships sailing in with cannons blasting and shore batteries returning the fire. Vessels must have been sunk in that harbor.

Only a short distance away was the area known as Massacre Beach. Could any treasure hunter standing on such a beach resist searching it for artifacts and relics that must surely have been lost in the slaughter? Do any of them still lie somewhere beneath its sands? Where?

As I studied the area, my eye was caught by an outcropping of coral protruding a few inches out of the water and ending abruptly where the sea washed upon dry land. It seemed logical to me that anything ever lost here in the sand could still be trapped by that coral that prevented high water from washing it back into the blue waters of the Caribbean.

Also, I thought of that barrier of anchors and the ships it had been designed to deter. If any of them had ever been sunk in the cove, storms could have hurled treasure from their wreckage onto this beach where objects might still lie captured by the coral. I walked to the edge of the water next to the coral outcropping and turned on my Master Hunter detector. After only a few scans, it sang out with that glorious "sound of money."

At a depth of about one foot, I dug into a shelf of solid coral that had become smooth from centuries of water and sand abrasion. When I moved my hand over the coral and failed to locate a target, I reasoned that it must be below the coral ledge. I scanned again and heard the detector frantically signaling the presence of something large and "valuable." Again, I dug my finger around in the hole, and sought to probe under the coral. My fingernails caught on something that moved.

This breathtaking discovery proved to be a Spanish icon made of pewter...the Virgin Mary holding the Christ child in her arms with halo rays adorning both heads. A Spanish coin discovered nearby and marked 1692, plus features of the icon, date the religious relic to the years just prior to 1700.

Learn from my success at finding the icon. "Reading" a site requires recognition of key features and the forces that may have acted upon them over the years. Beaches protected from winds that cause large waves are more popular than unprotected beaches. For instance, southward-facing beaches on the west coast of the United States are more protected from prevailing winds and heavy surf than beaches facing west or north.

As areas have grown more populated, former swimming beaches have disappeared or been permitted to erode. Land development and new business and industry have taken precedent over recreation and natural beauty. Breakwaters, harbor extensions, jetties and damming or otherwise diverting streams and rivers have destroyed once-popular play areas. Treasure lost there years ago, however, will remain forever — or, until it is found. Search out these treasure vaults and reap a harvest.

As experience accumulates, you will discover "mis-located" treasure in areas away from people. How did this happen? Perhaps this is where people used to congregate; it might once have been a swimming beach. Then, for some reason, the old beach was abandoned along with its treasure. Another reason is natural erosion that redeposits objects. Even though such action is seldom permanent, always keep in mind the forces that cause it to happen — and, watch for them in action. These forces do not occur accidentally, and they can create treasure vaults for you to find and unload.

Popular beaches usually feature fine, clean sand with a wide and gradual slope into the water. Remember that changes continually occur as a result of both man and nature. Popular play areas of yesterday may scarcely be recognizable as beaches today. Many such identifiable sections of "lost" beaches can be hunted profitably. Not all are still connected to the mainland; some are separated by lagoons and marshland. Some have been converted into bird and wildlife sanctuaries.

Obvious other places to search for beach treasure are man-made spots. Walk onto a beach and observe people at play. Watch children of all ages as they frolic. Then, when they tire of that activity, watch them scoot away. Coins fall from pockets...rings slip off of fingers...bracelets, necklaces and chains fall into the sand as young people play their games. Other more subtle games are being played on beach chairs and blankets, but wherever people relax, coins and jewelry are certain to fall into the sand.

Search around trails, walkways and boardwalks. Never pass up an opportunity to scan the base of seawalls and stone fences. People without chairs often camp by these structures where they can lean back. Always search under picnic tables and benches. Sure, you'll find lots of bottlecaps and pulltabs, but you will also find coins, toys and other valuable objects. Search around food stands, bath houses, shower stalls, dressing sheds and water fountains and under piers and stairs. Posts and other such obstacles are good "traps" where treasure can be found.

A piece of equipment often overlooked by the beginning beach hunter is the digging tool, since almost any type of digger can be used in loose beach sands. Some even use their hands, but I strongly counsel against this for several reasons, the first and foremost of these being the abundance of broken glass. In fact, I recommend gloves, at least one for the hand that you intend to do any digging.

144

Another reason for not depending upon hands alone as a digging tool is that the beach hunter cannot always expect to find targets in soft beach sand. Sometimes a sharp and hard-edged digger will be absolutely necessary.

In such dry, loose sand, however, scoops are reasonably good. A quick scoop, a few shakes and there's the find. In wet sand, however, scoops are just a waste of time. It takes too long to work damp sand out of a scoop, except in the water where onrushing surf can help clean wet sand from the scoop.

Other gear needed for beach hunting includes an assortment of pouches, a secure pocket for storing especially good finds and a place for personal items. If you've hunted for treasure at all, you probably already have some ideas about recovery pouches. Let me offer just a couple of suggestions for the beach:

— Place *all* detected items in a pouch; carefully inspect your finds occasionally and discard trash properly. When I find an especially valuable article, I return to my vehicle or camp to stow it properly.

— Use care in handling rings with stones. Often, mountings corrode during exposure. Examine jewelry with your pocket magnifier; when a mounting shows corrosion, handle that ring with extra caution.

— A fastener on a pouch is not a necessity on the beach unless you lay your pouch down carelessly or let it bounce around in your car.

— Pouches should be waterproof to prevent soiling your clothes and sturdy enough to hold plenty of weight.

— Many pouch styles can be mounted on a belt. I often wear a web-type belt carrying a canteen and an extra pouch or two.

Concerning clothing, the best advise is to dress comfortably. But, protect yourself against the elements you're sure to encounter on the beach. Obviously, you'll want to keep warm in the winter and cool in the summer, but I caution you to shade exposed skin areas to protect against sun and wind burn. In warm weather I wear shorts or lightweight trousers, a light (but long-sleeved) shirt, socks and comfortable shoes or sneakers. I wear a wide-brimmed cotton hat with some sort of neck shield. Even when hunting only on the beach, I'm always prepared to get wet. Sometimes an attractive low place in the sand will be yielding recoveries, and I must be prepared to follow it right into the water.

Winds, Tides and Weather

Wouldn't it be great if the ocean suddenly receded several feet, leaving your favorite hunting beach high and dry? You could walk right out and recover lost treasure so much more easily. Well, the ocean does recede slightly every day during low tide. This exposes more beach to be searched and also makes more shallow surf area available.

Listen regularly to weather reports and forecasts to learn of prevailing winds. Strong offshore (outgoing) winds will lower the water level and reduce size and force of breakers. Such offshore winds also spread out sand at the water's edge, reducing the amount that lies over the blanket of treasure. On the other hand, incoming wind and waves tend to pile sand up, causing it to increase in depth. Pay attention to winds and tides, especially during storms.

Storms often transfer treasure from deep water vaults to shallower locations. Plan a beach search immediately following a squall. If you are hardy enough, try working during the storm itself. Always remember that extremes in weather, wind and tides can cause unproductive beaches to become productive. Storms play havoc with beach sands. Fast-running currents that drain a beach can wash deep gullies in the sand...gullies to bring you closer to the blanket of treasure.

Sand Formations

Another reason for working beaches immediately after a storm is that the beach continually reshapes and protects itself. Sands shift normally to straighten the beachfront and present the least possible shoreline to the sea's continuous onslaught. During storms, beach levels decrease as sand washes out to form underwater bars which blunt the destructive force of oncoming waves. Following the storm, waves return this sand to the beach.

146

Look for tidal pools and long, water-filled depressions on the beach. Any areas holding water should be investigated since these low spots put you closer to the blanket of treasure. As the tide recedes, watch for streams draining back into the ocean. These will locate low areas where you can get your a detector's searchcoil closer to the treasure.

Since shorelines and beaches are continually being reshaped, you must be observant. One key to success is establishing permanent tide and sand markers. Such markers can be a piling or structure readily visible at any time. Ideally, your water marker will be somewhat submerged during both high and low tides. Checking this marker lets you measure water depth at all times to learn if the water is rising or falling.

Grid Searching

When searching a large area of beach with a metal detector, you should clearly define your area of search and systematically scan every square foot. There are many grid methods to use, some simple, some elaborate. The simplest, perhaps, is to guide on your previous tracks as you double back and forth. Using a stick or other object you can draw squares in the sand. Work the first square completely and then draw an adjoining square and work it.. These methods work if others don't destroy your tracks and lines as fast as you make them.

When selecting a beach on which to walk your grid pattern, seek one where you earlier observed a cut forming perpendicular to the waterline. High tides or waves pouring back into the ocean form these cuts, usually at low spots that have resulted from previous storms. Remember, cuts are important to you because they bring you closer to treasure; also, coins and jewelry washing off a beach are pushed into these cuts by streams of draining water.

Scanning Tips

Do not race across the sand with your searchcoil waving in front of you. *Slow down!* Work methodically in a preplanned pattern. Unless you are in a hurry and seek only shallow, recently lost treasure, reduce scan speed to about one foot per second. Let the searchcoil just skim the sands and keep it level throughout the length of a sweep. Overlap each sweep by advancing your searchcoil about one-half its diameter. Always scan in a straight line. This improves your ability to maintain correct and uniform searchcoil height, helps eliminate the "upswing" at the end of each sweep and improves your ability to overlap in a uniform manner, thus minimizing skips.

Don't ignore either very loud or very faint detector signals. Always determine the source. If a loud signal seems to come from a can or other large object, remove it and scan the spot again. When you hear a very faint signal, scoop out some sand to get your searchcoil closer to the target and scan again. If the signal has disappeared, scan the sand you scooped out. You may have detected a very small target. It might be only a BB, but at least you'll know what caused the signal.

Remember. Your metal detector will *never lie to you*. When it gives a signal, something is there.

The matter of trash on a beach is one that daily becomes more urgent to all of us beachcombers. I refer especially to plastic trash that is more than just unsightly. Fish and sea birds become entangled in six-pack rings; sea turtles mistake plastic bags for jelly fish and swallow them; birds peck at plastic pellets and try to feed them to their young. Similar harm results from countless other plastic items that are carelessly discarded on our nation's beaches every day. What can a beachcomber do about it?

Most THers carry out the metal trash they dig because we all benefit from its removal. But, what about non-metallic trash? Certainly, none of us carries around a container large

Discovery by the author of this valuable 17th-century Spanish icon in the surf of Guadaloupe is described on Pages 142-43 of this book.

enough to hold all the plastic trash and broken glass we find in only a few hours. Let's join together to help, however, and dispose properly of as much trash as we can. We perform a service not only for all beachcombers and sun worshipers but for sea creatures and bird life as well. How about it...can't we join together and help one another?

Sea Stories

One of the great thrills of beach hunting is that "big one" that always awaits...your chance to strike it rich. I'm very serious when I suggest that you should always be on the alert for treasure stories and legends. Please don't waste good money on a "treasure map," but don't ignore those tales of missing treasures...of great losses and "almost" or partial recoveries. Not only will this add excitement to your hobby, but the stories sometimes prove to be true!

Before you spend too much time seeking the mythical "pot o' gold," however, you should attempt to verify the sea story you are following. Major concerns before you get yourself seriously involved in tracking legends are, first, to make certain that the treasure ever actually existed; then, to locate the precise spot where it is rumored to have been lost or where it was only partially recovered. Remember that beaches run for miles and that names of various areas can change regularly. Also, the appearance of beaches change. Erosion may take years to alter a beach radically, but storms can transform its appearance in just a few hours.

Investigate stories and legends before ever turning on your metal detector. Check newspapers, police records, historical societies, local coin shops. Uncover sufficient information to

This THer is hunting on the beach with the famous Garrett Sea Hunter metal detector which has been involved in many great underwater discoveries.

convince yourself beyond the shadow of a doubt that the facts are correct. Then, you can pursue the tale, knowing that what you are searching for actually exists. When you locate unusual treasures on the beach, look more closely at nearby land and sea areas; you may have located a sunken treasure ship!

Some Final Tips

Schedule your beachcombing expeditions according to current (hourly) weather reports. Stay alert to weather forecasts and go prepared to withstand the worst.

Plan your treasure hunting expedition. Make a list of all you will need the day *before* you make the trip and check all gear carefully before you leave.

Always put *batteries* at the head of your list (see above). And, always check your batteries first if your detector should stop working. Some hobbyists take these longer-life batteries for granted and expect them to last forever. Believe me, they won't. You'd be amazed at how many *broken* detectors can be "repaired" with new batteries.

Take along a friend, if possible. If you go alone, leave word where you'll be. Always carry identification that includes one or more telephone numbers or persons to call (with a quarter for the pay phone taped to the list). Your personal doctor's name should be on this list.

Be wary of driving in loose sand. Carry along a tow rope and a shovel. You may need someone to pull you out of trouble, or you may have to dig ramps for your wheels if a tow vehicle isn't handy.

If there are no regulations to the contrary, you may want to search among crowds. But, don't annoy anyone. Angering the wrong person can result in immediate trouble, or you may find a complaint filed against you personally and the THing fraternity in general. You certainly wouldn't want to cause a beach to be put of limits for metal detecting.

Whenever possible, return any find to its owner. Try to oblige when someone asks your help in recovering a lost article. It might be feasible for you to loan them your detector and teach them how to use it. Who knows? You might add a

152

new member to our brotherhood. When helping look for a lost article, it's a good idea to keep its owner close by throughout the search so that they will know whether you succeed or not. If you can't find the article, get their name or address; you might find it another day.

Do not enter posted or "No trespassing" beaches without obtaining permission. Even in states where you are certain that all beaches are open to the public, do not search fenced or posted areas without permission. Never argue with a "loaded shotgun;" leave such property owners to themselves.

Finally, remember that a modern metal detector is a wonderful scientific instrument. It searches beneath the sand, where you cannot see. It is always vigilant about the presence of metal. But, no detector can "do it all." You must develop powers of observation that keep you attentive to what a detector cannot see. Watch for the unusual! Sometimes you'll visually locate money, marketable sea shells or other valuables. The real benefit of developing keen powers of observation, however, is to enable you to enjoy the glories of the beach to their fullest and never to overlook the signposts pointing to detectable treasure.

As you scan along the waterline and observe the sands under the water, you may eye a coin shining in the water. Check the spot with your metal detector. Perhaps you found only a freshly dropped coin, or it could be the top layer of much greater treasure. And, how about that rock outcropping, the gravel or shells peeking through the sand, that accumulation of debris...any of these might mark the location of a glory hole. Remain alert and be rewarded!

There's treasure to be found near the water! And, vast amounts are waiting...enough for all. I sincerely hope that you'll join the rest of us beachcombers in searching for this lost and hidden wealth. When you do, perhaps I'll see you on the beach!

13 – Looting Davy Jones' Treasure Locker...

Surf Hunting

ade out into the ocean...get away from the others...and find some *real* treasure! What's that? You say that you already hunt on the beach...you've already proven how productive it is...you're aware of the Spanish galleons but you don't scuba dive.

You're not alone! It's surprising how few THers ever venture into the surf...which is a blessing for those of us who do...because this is one of the richest of all areas for seeking lost treasure with a metal detector. Out in the surf is where you will find treasure hunters who are a bit more adventurous...a lot more successful...and a great deal wealthier.

The ratio of land hunters to water hunters is easily 100 to 1! Isn't that amazing when you consider the treasure to be found? Of course, water hunting seems to require a few more skills which we will discuss, and there are perceived dangers you won't find on land such as stinging jellyfish. Believe me, however, when I say that about the only way you'll ever get tangled up with one of those nasty fellows is to work with your eyes shut.

If you could search just one small spot in the surf off a crowded beach every day for the rest of your life, you'd *never* empty the treasure vault just lying there. You see, this vault is being replenished continually by ocean waves and tides — night and day — month after month after month.

What exactly is surf hunting? Where does beach hunting end and surf hunting begin?

Visualize, if you will, the seashore divided into three sections or "zones." Zone Number 1 is the actual beach that you may have searched so many times...that sandy spot between parking lot or road and the tidal mark. Sometimes it stretches across an island from bay to ocean. But, the "beach" generally stays dry except during storms and flood tides.

Zone Number 3 is the deep water expanse stretching out as far as the eye can see. It's where the sunken galleons lie...where there is truly great treasure to be found by underwater divers with special equipment. But, it's a place for scuba gear, underwater detectors and divers with training.

Zone Number 2 belongs to the surf hunter. It's our treasure vault...the area where a beginner with the right equipment can be successful. It's the shallow surf from the foamy water's edge out into the ocean five feet deep or at least as deep as you feel safe standing on your feet. Here's where treasure awaits your keen eyes and probing searchcoil — coins and jewelry, wealth of all kinds.

The tale of one such pair of keen eyes on the beautiful beaches of Grand Cayman was related by my good friend Robert Marx. This surf hunter spotted something shining on the sandy bottom in shallow water. To his astonishment it turned out to be a gold cross covered with diamonds. Without telling anyone, he returned later and really struck it rich. Using only his hand to fan away thin layers of sand in the shallow water, he recovered a fantastic cache of treasure, including a large bar of platinum dated 1521, various bars of silver bullion, a silver bracelet in the form of a serpent covered with emeralds and a large gold ring bearing the arms of the Ponce de Leon family. Since there is no evidence of a shipwreck ever having occurred in the area, the treasure — perhaps the booty of a conquistador — was probably buried ashore and washed out into the shallow sea as the beach eroded.

Few are this lucky — and, believe me, luck is important to the treasure hunter, no matter how great his skill and training — but treasures await all of us in the surf, ready to sing out in response to the signal of a modern metal detector.

I must also point out that in addition to the increased monetary rewards of surf hunting you'll receive physical and spiritual benefits. You just can't help but be healthier at the end of a long and vigorous hunting session. I always feel terrific following a day in the surf. I've spent weeks searching the surf of Caribbean beaches in hot and humid weather. Yet, following a day's hunting of six to eight hours, all that is needed to refresh me for the next day is a hot shower, a good meal and a full night's sleep.

You don't fatigue when you work the surf – even in the 100-degree heat of the tropics. The sea breeze, the water all around you, the excitement of the hunt and the thrill of discovery...all of these contribute to a sense of pleasure, satisfaction and self worth.

There are several major differences you will find between THing on the park – or, even on the beach – and searching in the surf:
   – *Where to search;*
   – *What to look for and expect to find;*
   – *How to recover your targets;*
   – *Dealing with the water itself.*

It's Number Three, above, *recovery* that separates the water hunter from the land hunter...the men from the boys...the surf hunter from the beach hunter...the sheep from the goats.

Equipment that you will need in the surf will, of course, depend upon whether you work in shallow or deep water. Shallow surf is water depth that permits you to dig with a hand tool, a scoop or some sort of digger—in other words, at arm's length. Deep water surfing is hunting in depths of about five feet, or the maximum depth you can safely wade in the water without swimming or floating.

Your choice of retrieving tools will depend upon soil conditions and personal preferences. In sandy areas, a scoop is fast. If the soil is muddy or made of hardened clay, you will need some kind of digger. In deep water, a long-handled scoop is required to retrieve your finds.

When the water grows colder, hip or chest-high waders and suitable underclothing will keep you warm and dry. When wearing waders, be alert or else you may bend too far.

Suddenly, you'll find yourself wearing "convertible" gear; your waders have been converted into a wet suit! Wearing a waist or chest belt over waders can reduce the amount of water that comes in.

No matter what type of treasure pouch or pouches you use, they must close tightly. Water-hunting treasure pouches must have a secure flap covering. Some surfers use a sturdy open-weave bag or pouch with zipper or drawstring. Whatever equipment your ingenuity comes up with, keep it in good shape. Don't lose valuables through holes! It's a good idea to have several pockets that let you separate treasure and trash. But, whatever you do, never discard trash without carefully examining every piece. You may have inadvertently placed a good find in the trash pocket. Also, that item that looked so corroded and unrecognizable may turn out to be a valuable object. When in doubt about any find, take it home for closer examination, even an electrolytic bath for cleaning. A broach worth more than a million dollars was thought to be just a worthless piece of junk jewelry when first pulled from the surf. Cleaning revealed its true worth!

Surf Hunting Detectors

When you use a land detector in the surf, you must absolutely prevent the control housing from getting wet. No land detector can be as efficient as a submersible detector designed to be used in the water. There are submersible models such as the Garrett Sea Hunter XL500 that were designed especially for maximum performance in the water. Their design prevents water from seeping into the control housing and searchcoils. This detector is equipped with underwater headphones.

I don't recommend a land detector for working water more than knee deep. If fact, I don't recommend using a land detector for any extended water hunting. It's too easy to become lax and forget about your detector. And, believe me, when you're in the water all of your equipment requires *constant* attention. I recall once while working the water's edge on a beautiful Cozumel beach, I was having good success. Because I was digging in dry sand, I wasn't paying particular attention to the action of nearby waves. When I stopped scanning to recover my next find, I carelessly laid my detector too near the water. Splash! Here came a high wave to give my control housing a good bath, and searching for the day was ended...at least, with that detector!

Searchcoils

If you question whether your searchcoil is waterproof, don't hesitate to ask your metal detector dealer or manufacturer. All searchcoils manufactured by Garrett are fully submersible, but I don't know if all searchcoils on the market today can be safely submerged.

Most land searchcoils are buoyant. You must add weight to give the searchcoil either neutral or slightly negative buoyancy. A small sand bag or other weight can be attached to the top of your searchcoil, and some surf hunters fashion specially shaped weights made of lead or cement. Others pour lead into the stem itself to keep from adding extra drag and water resistance. Make certain that any lead weight and/or other metal is kept at least eight inches above the searchcoil. A weight of from one to three pounds is usually necessary.

I prefer that my detector float somewhat vertically so that the searchcoil "bobbles" near the bottom. This keeps the handle near at hand. When I have recovered a find, I need only to reach over and take hold of the detector handle to continue my search. Some hobbyists recommend letting the stem and searchcoil float on the surface during recovery. This involves extra work and effort because you have to reach up to grab the handle and then force the searchcoil down to the bottom each time you stop to inspect or recover a target. To achieve the proper "float" and angle, it may be necessary to add buoyancy material such as cork or styrofoam to the upper end of the stem. Tape the cable to the stem at a point near the searchcoil to prevent it from snagging on objects.

What about discrimination for a water detector? First of all, THing books — mine as well as others — probably contain more information and recommendations about discrimination than any other subject. Some say discriminating metal detectors are practically worthless in the water; others swear by them. I'm talking about experienced and successful surf hunters now, in addition to writers.

Since I fit in both categories, I urge you to study this literature and make up your own mind. I know that surf hunters with discriminating detectors sometimes find it very difficult and frustrating to work heavy trash areas. Some even refuse to work areas with a great deal of trash, preferring more productive sites. I recommend that while you not seek out locations with trash, that you not avoid them either.

Some surf hunters will tell you not to use discrimination because you will lose silver and gold chains. It's not just discrimination that sometimes causes these items to be lost; it is also their shape. Eddy currents must be generated on the surface of metal for the object to be detected. Since chains have such a tiny surface compared with their mass, these items present a poor target for detection. Consequently, you will locate about as many chains using a normal amount of discrimination as you will if you don't use any — especially if the gold or silver content is high.

If you were to ask me to recommend a discrimination setting, I would encourage you to set discrimination to zero — to accept all targets and to dig everything. That is the only way to be certain of locating all rings and all possible chains. I believe that many such items have been missed because pulltab discrimination was used. Many surf hunters have told me they were successful because they do dig junk. Possibly — just possibly — you could set discrimination to reject iron hair pins, if they are numerous, but I recommend no more discrimination than that level.

The dedicated treasure hunter always seeks out sites through research. Beyond that, experience must be the teacher. Inquiring and attentive hobbyists will continually pick up ideas that will often rescue them when studying a new area. My books and those of other treasure hunters list numerous research sources where both general and specific leads can be found for searching surf locations with a metal detector. As the hobbyist researches these various sources, techniques and abilities will improve. That's why I urge anyone to apply himself or herself to water hunting for at least a full year before attempting to judge this aspect of THing. And, when you seek to carry out the recommended research, I implore you not to be haphazard or sloppy. Be diligent and methodical; your progress and success will amaze you.

Scanning Tips

Here's a phenomenon to observe while surf hunting: Remember the science classes of your school days when you learned about diffraction or the "bending" of light? This occurs when light passes through a water/air boundary. An underwater object such as your searchcoil will thus appear to be in a different place from where it actually sits. Until you get used to it, this sighting error may cause you to misjudge the location of your searchcoil in relation to your scoop.

When you're working a popular area and do not find *any* pulltabs, someone may have just worked the area thoroughly. Since some hunters dig everything, or at least use minimum discrimination, they will remove everything, including pulltabs.

When working in surfs with rough wave action, always work sideways to the oncoming breakers. You need to present as little of yourself to the body-flattening waves as possible. Don't forget, either, that some waves are considerably larger than others.

When scanning, keep the searchcoil near the bottom and lightly skim over the sand. If you hold the searchcoil very far above the bottom, you will lose detection depth. If you drag the searchcoil through the sand, you will be expending energy you need for a full day's scanning.

Dig all signals, regardless of magnitude! Some suggest *not* digging large signals. They reason that large detector signals merely indicate surface trash. But, treasure is sometimes found directly beneath surface trash. I know of a surf hunter who found a gold ring after he moved a "loud" tin can.

On hot sunny days wear a wide-brimmed cotton hat. Occasionally dunk it in the water and pull it back down over your head. You'll be surprised hoe cool you'll remain even during temperatures well over 90 degrees. I've worked all day for days on end in very hot climates with absolutely no problems. When not out in deep water, I wear long-sleeved shirts with the collar turned up. I place a handkerchief under my hat and let the loose end shade my neck. In a surplus store I found a sun "shield" to protect my neck from the sun.

It's best not to show your good finds to strangers. Let them think you're digging up junk and pulltabs, and they will leave you alone. I like tots, and you may also, but if you don't want to be pestered by them, don't give them your pennies or other coins you don't want. Whenever I forget and begin to give coins away to children, I'm soon covered up with others wanting their share. Nothing wrong with sharing or with charity in general, certainly, but these children will distract you when you need to devote all your attention to finding treasure.

One final bit of advice: Remember, you plan to search the surf to find the lost treasure of others, not your own valuables. Leave all of *your* jewelry at home so some other surf hunter won't be scooping it up tomorrow.

Good luck in your surf hunting. If this chapter has stirred your interest, I refer you to the other Ram publications listed on the Order Blank at the end of this book. You can learn even more from them. I sincerely hope that you'll enjoy hunting for treasure in the surf with a metal detector as much as I have and that someday I can see you in the surf!

Underwater Hunting

Considering the vast amount of wealth lost in the ocean, it seems likely that a good percentage of all treasure hunters have *dreamed* of going after their share. Of those who think about it, however, probably no more than five percent ever even get their feet wet. Searching for underwater treasure requires greater skills and offers more rewards than any other type. Yet, the *thoughts* (or fears) of water hunting and the required skills and equipment (scuba gear, etc.) that is mandatory keep most people safely on land...and away from vast treasures that could be theirs.

What are underwater treasure recovery dreams made of? First, there is the discovery of a bronze cannon buried in the sand and refusing to surrender to the corroding effects of salt water. Next to it a hand slowly and carefully fans the sand to uncover an ancient treasure chest. Just a slight tug and the lid swings up to expose gleaming golden doubloons! While we all know that it "ain't that easy," isn't it nice to dream?

Treasure is scattered *everywhere* on the ocean floors of the world...most of it relatively close to land. Largely unexplored regions hide many fortunes which can be claimed by those with determination to seek them out. In fact, man has been seeking sunken treasure for thousands of years. Down through the centuries records explicitly record attempts by divers to recover sunken treasure.

Other than during wartime, most ships meet disaster in shallow water. Reefs or shoals have ripped the bottom out of thousands of ships, spilling cargo into shallow water. Along the coastline of several Central and South American countries shallow reefs parallel the mainland. The remains of numerous

163

vessels lie hidden in the ever-growing coral that relentlessly strives to conceal these sunken riches.

We explored one such wreck site off South America that was visibly marked by a stack of more than a dozen coral-encrusted cannon. It was strange to see these cannon stacked like cordwood, almost totally concealed by coral growth. How did the cannon become stacked like that? Perhaps the vessel was transporting cannon barrels and the seamen had stored them in one location on the ship. When the ship struck the razor-sharp coral reef, it broke up and quickly sank to the bottom. Over the ensuing decades the wooden ship succumbed to the teredo, leaving the ship's cannon cargo lying exposed on the bottom. There were no other visible signs of the ship except for an occasional cannonball.

When we scanned the bottom with our metal detectors, it was a different story. The "eyes" of the detectors pierced through the coral to locate hundreds of metal objects that human eyes could not see. Using rock picks to hack our way through the coral, we discovered more cannon balls, various pieces of iron, and numerous pieces of eight. Sometimes the silver cobs came out in clumps of coral. When the detector indicated that the detected metal object was larger than a single coin, we would hack out large chunks of coral. Later examination of these pieces of coral revealed numerous cobs that had been bound together by the rock-like growth.

Because of the growing amount of publicity that was given to numerous major discoveries in the early-to-mid 1980s, I hastened to publish the first edition of my book *Treasure Recovery from Sand and Sea*, which I completely updated and revised just a couple of years ago. If you're seriously interested in underwater exploration and recovery, I urge you to study this book. Then you'll want to learn more about diving, underwater archaeology and a host of other subjects.

If you are thinking about hopping into the ocean and discovering an ancient shipwreck by quickly spotting its hull, superstructure and, perhaps, even its *mast*, forget it! You won't find these unless you discover a one-in-a-thousand vessel that was, by some quirk of nature, quickly preserved under protective sand and silt. Then, the day before you dove, it would be necessary for a record-setting hurricane to blast a path through the area, leaving your ship uncovered. *Not likely!*

The remains of most old ships are scarcely recognizable as ships. Most wood will have succumbed long ago to the ocean's elements and creatures. Some assorted objects made of metal may remain, but they will probably be hidden or otherwise covered with sand, silt or marine growth. Nature seeks to return all man-made objects to their natural state — wood and similar organic substances, back to the soil whence they came...metals, like iron, back to magnetite or other ferrous material.

That's why so much study and research is necessary before any diving is attempted.

Metal detectors are valuable tools for underwater THers. They penetrate sand, mud, clay, coral and other marine growth, stone, rock and other non-metallic substances. Metal detectors can be used to locate wreck sites and objects such as the coins vital to dating a wreck. They can lead a treasure hunter to gold, silver, pewter, bronze, brass and other metallic treasures and help to check a "cleaned" area to make certain that all treasures, ship's rigging and other artifacts have been recovered.

Metal detectors offer "x-ray" scanning to help locate hidden metal objects. Detectors will locate single objects as small as a coin to a distance of 12 inches or more outward from the searchcoil's bottom surface. A mass of coins and other metal objects can be detected to a distance of 4 to 6 feet. Larger objects like cannon and anchors can be detected to a distance of about 8 to 10 feet.

Submersible and self-contained metal detectors feature electronics, controls, indicators, batteries and the searchcoil mounted within a specially designed, submersible, water-tight housing. A suitable handle arrangement allows the searchcoil to be maneuvered over an area to be searched. Indicator lights, a visual indicator (moving pointer or liquid crystal) and an audible device (usually dynamic speaker-type headphones or a piezo electric crystal) are the detection-alert devices that report the presence of metal to a diver.

Self-contained batteries that can power a detector for 10 or more hours are usually rechargeable. Some models are stem-mounted, while others are convertible. The control housing is designed to be attached to the stem (stem-mounted) or belt-mounted to waist, arm or leg. When the housing is body-mounted, a short handle attached to the searchcoil allows the coil to be maneuvered over the search area.

The initial search for the site can be conducted by a diver (or divers) scanning an area according to a search-grid network. Since searchcoils will not "reach out" laterally, they must be scanned directly above as much of the target area as possible. Because most ships carried considerable metal, however, even a cursory scan of an area can often locate a wreck site. Any methodical grid search is satisfactory, but the expanding circle method provides the most uniform searching pattern. A cord or rope is wound around a suitable spool. The spool is anchored and the diver slips his hand through a loop in the end of the cord. The diver swims around the spool, scanning the detector searchcoil ahead. As the rope unwinds, it guides the diver in a controlled expanding circle.

A metal detector can speed up almost any search for a shipwreck with concealed treasure. When a sonar device locates a ballast pile, a quick scan with a metal detector will reveal whether metal objects are concealed within the ballast.

Metal detectors with a built-in discrimination system are more versatile than non-discriminating types. For quickly surveying a site to locate only coins and other non-ferrous objects, the discriminating type should be used. This is a fast

Divers with the proper equipment are remarkably successful in discovering treasures that lie hidden beneath the depths of the world's oceans and lakes.

method to determine if the ship's cargo included treasure. Since non-corrosive metals survive longer than iron objects, identifying stamps, insignias and other markings were usually affixed to these metals. Locating such pieces can hasten identification of the wreck.

When a sunken ship is totally or even partially encrusted and there is not time for a complete excavation, a discriminating metal detector can locate only non-ferrous objects, such as coins, jewelry, navigation instruments and dinnerware. A metal detector with interchangeable searchcoils can be used another way. With a small searchcoil you can detect and precisely pinpoint smaller objects to speed up retrieval. Although not particularly necessary in sand, precise pinpointing in concrete- like coral can minimize hacking and chiseling. When most non- ferrous shallow objects have been recovered, a larger, more deepseeking searchcoil can locate bigger objects at greater depths.

Should you be fortunate enough to find your ship in sand, the first phase of recovery work will require only your hands. Slowly fan the sand away to create a cavity. As lighter materials flow away, heavier items such as coins, jewelry, china and other objects with a higher specific gravity will remain in place. In currents you may need to anchor yourself over the spot by holding an anchor rope, or grasping an underwater object. Don't try to hold on to coral unless you wear gloves; the glass-like substance can penetrate skin to cause pain and swelling. A ping pong paddle or a child's bounce-the-ball paddle makes fanning easier. A water jet can easily remove silt and light overburden.

Diver searches floor of Red Sea at top; below is the famed Emerald Cross and other jewelry recovered off Bermuda from a 16th-century Spanish shipwreck.

Specialized Instruments

If funds allow, specialized instruments can aid in your search for a shipwreck. These include magnetometers and gradiometers, side-scan sonar, sub-bottom profilers and robot and manned submersibles. If it is known or suspected that your ship contained a considerable quantity of large iron objects such as cannon and anchors, a magnetometer will locate the magnetic mass by sensing the increase in the earth's magnetic field concentration. Of course, iron objects such as steel drums and other discarded iron trash will also create a detectable concentration of the earth's field, causing you to spend time investigating false leads.

Side scan sonar and sub-bottom profilers are capable of revealing remarkable detail of sunken objects. These instruments are not infallible, but they permit scanning a wide swath of ocean floor. Manned robots using video scanning were used to locate the *Titanic*. Their value remains unquestioned, not only when used in the original search, but also during all phases of surveying, mapping, and excavation.

Whether visual or electronic scanning techniques are used, grid-search methods are essential. Haphazard searching wastes time, money and resources. Many grid-search methods have been developed over the years.

Site Identification

Now that you've found a wreck, is it really the one you have searched for? You must be certain because an extensive conglomerate of ballast, cannonballs, perhaps a few cannon, cargo, countless pieces of copper, lead, iron, bottles, pottery and tons of mud and silt (and perhaps tons of forbidding coral growth) will be found at most old shipwreck sites. You will be spending, perhaps, months and years excavating the site. What a pity it would be if the wreck contained not one ounce of treasure!

You must always determine beforehand whether any other salvage has been carried out. Possibly, the salvage data can help establish the ship's identity. Coins and ingots provide conclusive evidence, but these may not be encountered until later in the site excavation process. The ship's dimensions, number of decks, type of sheathing used, country of origin of cannon and hundreds of other clues are important in identification. Barry Clifford was able to identify his shipwreck immediately and without a doubt. He discovered what he believed to be the *Whidah*, a pirate ship that sank off the coast of Massachusetts in 1717. From the site he pulled a large bell which had the ship's name clearly cast into its side.

Surveying and Mapping

Before proceeding to excavate, the site should be surveyed and mapped. Aside from archaeological considerations, much useful data can be obtained. Your task will be easier if the ship is not scattered over a wide area and if the ocean bottom is sandy. In heavy coral areas, your job will be much more difficult and require hand chisels, sledge hammers and, possibly, pneumatic tools.

Determining the size of area over which a ship's remains are strewn will help plan future excavation since more time may be needed if the wreck is not contained in a small area. You'll need to know the type equipment needed. Your lease should clearly define the extent of your site. It is important to know the ship's orientation by determining bow and stern. You may want to excavate the stern first. The richest treasure, plus the private wealth of officers and passengers, can usually be found here. Silverware, china, and other more valuable artifacts are also more likely to be found in the stern section.

Site Excavation

If you've made it this far, congratulations! Excavation has finally begun, and you're much closer to your bank's deposit window. Excavation methods range from simply plucking a gold escudo out of the sand to managing giant airlifts and blasters. Select and use those that best suit your salvage job.

A "center" of the wreck site may contain most of the ship's cargo and other valuable artifacts. Try to establish an underwater grid system and keep it in place throughout your entire project for documenting the exact location of discoveries. The grid method is the most widely used on both land and underwater excavation sites. A grid pattern, built of non-metallic pipe (if metal detectors are to be used) is generally built on a compass alignment basis with equal size squares of five to ten feet. As objects are excavated within each square, their location is indicated on a corresponding chart.

Much simpler and less time consuming is an azimuth circle system. Such a circle is mounted on a brass rod and driven into the bottom near the center of the wreck site. If the wreck is scattered over a large area, it may be necessary to place an azimuth circle at several points. The azimuth circle is aligned with magnetic north. A small chain (or non-metallic, non-stretchable rope), with distance calibration marks along the entire length of the chain, is connected to the center of the brass rod with a collar to permit the chain to be rotated 360 degrees. When the chain is stretched to the object to be mapped, compass bearing on the azimuth circle and the distance to the object are recorded.

At sites where the bottom is uneven or with considerable marine growth and possibly large mounds of covered ballast, ship's cargo and various debris, standard grid techniques may not be feasible. In such cases, you can devise a "floating" grid network. Such a network should be securely anchored and be kept aloft by air-filled containers.

The various small personal tools you may need include a flashlight, hammer or sledge, chisel, crowbar and geologist's pick. Various floats, pouches, net bags and large containers will also be needed. Lifting big or heavy artifacts requires lift bags and other buoyancy devices.

Final Comments

The waters of the earth constitute a tremendous treasure bank. There is wealth to be found, and treasure hunters will always seek their share. Thrills await you when you join the ranks of beach, surf and underwater hunters. The sheer joy of the chase itself will come first...just scanning your detector over a sandy beach or in splashing surf. Then, what a delight awaits when you find your first coin! When mere nickels and quarters become so commonplace that they cease to excite, you'll begin searching for rare and more valuable coins and rings, jewelry, relics and sunken treasure.

Your determination will stimulate more research and literally force you to discover history and to experience its fascination. Whether young or old, male or female, you'll not turn back after you find your first treasure. This chapter is designed to guide you to the path you'll want to take. Start right, and you'll follow it successfully!

One final admonition before we begin...*always enjoy yourself and try to have fun*!

Gar Starrett is a fictional character I created to tell about some of the exciting treasure hunts in which my friends and I have participated. In each of the novels featuring him, Gar makes the same statement about treasure hunting. His observation is so pertinent that every treasure hunter should heed it:

"If nobody gets hurt or spends money he or she can't afford, every treasure hunt is a genuine pleasure!"

I couldn't have said it better myself!

Gold Hunting

W hile it is impossible to guarantee success in the prospecting field, I can assure you that if you follow just *three* basic rules you can be virtually certain of finding at least some gold or other precious metal with a metal detector.

Rule 1 – Choose the correct *type* of detector for prospecting.

Rule 2 – Use this detector with patience.

Rule 3 – Hunt patiently in areas where gold has already proved its presence.

These rules come from my close friend, veteran prospector Roy Lagal, who has been successful in finding gold with a metal detector for many more years than we have known each other. Most of this chapter represents his wisdom and experience.

Now let's examine the three rules.

Number One, of course, requires the most explanation. What is the *correct* type of detector? This doesn't necessarily mean some particular brand or model...although Roy obviously favors the Garrett instruments which he has helped me to develop over the years.

In the past, as technology and salesmanship prevailed. There were (too) many detector types introduced – with the unfortunate emphasis on salesmanship. Letters such as BFO, TR, IB, RF, MPD, TGC, etc. (to seeming *endlessness*) described the various instruments. Each type claimed to have its differences and peculiarities and, of course, its infinite advantages. And, it is true that some manufacturers and promoters misled many metal detector hobbyists. Unfortunately, the THers became convinced that they could rush out into a gold-producing area with *any* type of detector and find nuggets and placer gold. It is possible that those individuals who manufactured and/or sold the so-called *gold-finding* detectors simply did not understand the limitations of their instruments. Let's hope that naivete alone explains the situation!

Even with the older detectors, however, some amateur prospectors found some gold. Yet, anyone who has been successful in the gold fields with an older detector has seen this success magnified through use of a proper modern instrument. My field testing and experiences conclusively prove the truth of that statement. Today we have the new universal computerized instruments with microprocessor controls that perform excellently in the gold fields, as in all other treasure hunting environments.

Today's modern detectors offer greatly expanded capabilities:

— Detection depth has been tremendously increased, particularly with the highly regarded 15 kHz "Groundhog" circuit;

— Ground mineral problems have been mostly overcome;

— Rapid and accurate identification of "hot rocks" is possible, even for the beginner.

As a result of extensive field and laboratory tests and careful electronic design and manufacturing techniques, detectors possessing very exacting metal/mineral locating and identifying characteristics are now being built. Using these tested and proven detectors, both professional and recreational prospectors are making rich strikes in previously unworked areas, unearthing nuggets similar to those found at the turn of the century.

And, all of the older detectors finally have something in common...they are totally and absolutely *obsolete*. Don't expect any kind of favorable results using any one of them.

In fact, it was apparent many years ago that the VLF (very low frequency) type of detector was best suited for analyzing small conductive nuggets and ore specimens as well as accomplishing the other gold-hunting tasks. All detectors manufactured today are essentially VLF instruments. The older detectors could differentiate between metal and mineral, but none of them offered a fraction of the depth possible with a modern instrument.

Now, when I use the word *modern* in talking about a metal detector I am referring primarily to an instrument with computerized circuitry and microprocessor controls. Detectors such as this with which I am familiar are our Grand Master Hunter CX III and II, the Master Hunter CX and the magnificent new GTA series, the most popular metal detectors ever introduced.

Garrett's Scorpion Gold Stinger does not contain a microprocessor, but it is completely modern in every other way, and its circuitry has been computer-designed. I hunt with the Stinger or the CX III, but under the proper circumstances I would expect to find nuggets with any of these computerized Garrett detectors (or even with the Freedom Ace that is so popular with beginners). Regardless of what type detector you choose, I hope that it is a modern one and that it offers a true non-motion All Metal mode and a full range of discrimination for all types of treasure hunting as well as ore sampling.

When you're comparing instruments before purchase, you often are exposed to "bench-testing." Now, used in its place and for the right purpose bench-testing is well and good. And, when you use this method to test an unfamiliar detector, the test will certainly tell you how far away from its searchcoil any particular detector can locate a coin or gold nugget. Yet how many coins or gold nuggets do you really expect to find out in the air in front of a searchcoil?

Roy has told me of one particular detector that performs magnificently in a bench test...coins and nuggets well over a foot away can be detected. Take it outdoors, however, scoop just a little wet sand over a penny or a gold ring and this particular detector can't locate either of them. What I'm suggesting is that you *field-test* an instrument before you get carried away about its capabilities. And, if you're going hunting for gold, you should test it in gold country. Since this is usually impractical, I urge that you listen to the recommendations of those metal detector experts whom you trust.

While theoretically possible, searching for nuggets could not really be accomplished with the older detectors...especially in areas with highly mineralized soils. Some of us wrote books describing how the search *should* be conducted, and some of you followed our instructions and even found nuggets. Yet, how many smaller nuggets did we leave behind? And, how often did we come home empty-handed? If you got discouraged, I don't blame you. So did I!

Perhaps you became so discouraged that you swore *never* to hunt for nuggets again with a metal detector. If you decided this, I strongly urge you to change your mind because *you don't know what you're now missing out on!*

Modern instruments with their precise ground balancing capabilities feature high sensitivity and can completely balance out *all* effects of negative mineralization. Hunting for nuggets in gold country can be just as effortless as searching a park for coins...as far as the effects of ground mineralization are concerned. Gold nuggets can be found amid mineralized rocks with ease.

How about "hot rocks?" Their importance may have been somewhat "oversold," but they exist nonetheless and must be considered. These pesky geologic freaks are simply rock specimens that are "mis-located;" i.e., they are out of place in the geological environment where you find them. Thus, your ground balanced detector may indicate that you have found a nugget.

Hot rock response is troublesome in some areas, but your gold hunting detector will not indicate its presence unless the hot rock is close to the searchcoil, a maximum distance roughly equal to the diameter of the searchcoil. If a detected target is "suspect," switch into the Discriminate mode (set to "zero" elimination) and pass back over the target. If the sound

178

decreases from the audio threshold level, the target is a rock or mineralized hot spot. If the audio remains the same or increases, investigate the target. It has some metallic content.

So much for Rule One. I confirm that Roy's advice on it is sound. I know many detector enthusiasts who have had success following that advice. Roy and I both wish that we could be as helpful on Rule Two.

Patience

You must have it. Learn to understand your detector fully and become proficient in its use. Take your time in the field and don't get in a hurry. Try not to get discouraged when results are disappointing. And, if all else fails, fall back on this tested prayer:

Lord, please give me patience, but be quick about it because I don't have time to wait!

Rule Three concerns where you start your search. You must utilize some research. No one can find gold or any other precious metal where they simply do not exist. Confine your searching to areas that are known to have produced gold until you have become very familiar with the telltale signs of mineral zones. And, even when you decide to strike out on your own into an untested area, rely heavily on Rule Two!

There are so many things that are now possible with modern electronic metal detectors! An entire vista has been opened up by truly dramatic technological improvements. Totally new areas of opportunity are being revealed to even the most veteran gold hunters. Novices are fortunate indeed to be able to begin their electronic prospecting careers with the 21st-century detectors that are available today.

If you're interested in finding gold with a metal detector, I suggest that you read Roy's new *Gold Panning is Easy* or *Modern Electronic Prospecting,* which he and I wrote about five years ago.

Can I really find gold with a metal detector?

This is the question that I hear most often from gold seekers who doubt their ability — or *anyone's* ability, for that matter — to find gold electronically.

The answer to that question is a most emphatic *Yes!* Roy and I have proved, many times over, the abilities of metal detectors for finding gold. ①

Unbelievable success can await you if you will use the *correct instrument,* conduct research thoroughly and employ the virtues of *wisdom* and patience. ③

Gold Panning

Panning for gold can be one of the most delightful methods of treasure hunting...as well as one of the least expensive...and most profitable. Plus, panning for gold gives you an excellent excuse to visit some of the most beautiful country in the United States.

And, all you need is a good gold pan! Remember the old prospector from the Western movies riding his decrepit burro across Monument Valley into a beautiful Hollywood sunset? All he had was a skillet or pie pan with which he scooped up gravel and panned for gold. Of course, he needed more equipment than that (a shovel or digging tool, certainly) but as far as the pan was concerned, the depiction is still more or less accurate.

And, modern pans have been designed that make recovering gold a much easier task than it was for the old-timers. You'll be amazed at how little even the finest one will cost!

Concerning your *excuse* to visit beautiful country, it's really more than that because you should never attempt to pan for gold except in areas where it has already been found. That might sound like a *Catch 22*, but it's an unwritten rule that even the most veteran prospectors follow. After all, proven gold country is so vast that it's always possible to find some good vacation area with *nearby* gold production!

Gold panning is simple! Basically, gold pans and gold panning methods have remained unchanged for centuries. Because gold is slightly more than 19 times as heavy as water, it will sink rapidly and is easily recovered by "panning." Various methods have been used since the earliest times with many different types of vessels employed over the years.

Yet, regardless of the vast span of time that gold has been coveted as wealth, the methods of recovering it by panning remain basically the same. Any type of jar, bowl or metal container or even any type of material, such as a blanket, can be used to recover the heavy metal. In water it can easily be panned, or sorted from the lighter rocks and dirt, because gold is heavier and tends to sink quickly down through all debris, finally coming to rest at the bottom. Gold can also be recovered by dry methods where water is not available; however, this "dry washing" or panning is not as efficient, and generally only the heavier pieces can be recovered without sophisticated equipment.

Simply stated, if you intend to seek gold in the field, it is vital that you have a good gold pan and that you understand its importance and know how to use it properly.

Pan designs have improved greatly since the old prospector's time. Today's gold pan is lighter in weight and offers greater speed in testing and classifying material. It is also easier to handle and provides safer, surer results, especially for the beginner. Absolutely no experience is required for a beginner to enjoy success in the first panning session.

During the gold rush days of the 19th and early 20th centuries, gold panning was more than hard work; it was back-breaking labor. Unless a panner was lucky, his efforts were usually not especially profitable. Today, however, gold panning is much easier for an individual and can even be more productive than it was for the 49ers. This has happened not only because of the increased price of gold but because of the modern gold pans now available.

Of course, I believe the finest and most effective gold pan today to be the Gravity Trap® gold pan. Invented by my friend Roy Lagal (U.S. Patent #4,162,969) and manufactured by my company, its effectiveness has been proven by worldwide success and acceptance. Made of unbreakable polypropylene, the pan is far lighter and easier to handle than the old metal pans. More importantly, the Gravity Trap pan has built-in gold traps in the form of sharp 90° riffles. These riffles are designed to trap particles of while allowing unwanted sand, rocks and gravel to be easily and quickly "panned-off."

The pan is forest green in color which has been proved in laboratory and field tests to show gold, garnets, precious gems and black sand better than other colors, including black. After only a little practice, a weekend or recreational placer miner using this new pan can work with equal or greater efficiency than the most proficient professional using old style metal pans or those of black plastic design.

Gold Pan Kit

Because Roy Lagal saw a pressing need for a totally complete — but lightweight and compact — prospecting kit, especially for hobbyists and beginning prospectors, Garrett designed the Gravity Tra p Gold Panning Kit. This handsomely packaged kit contains a 14 1/2-inch and a 10 1/2-inch Gravity Trap gold pan, a classifer (sieve) for sorting rocks and a suction bottle for retrieving small pieces of gold. With the individual pieces designed to fit compactly together the kit carries easily, completely serving the needs of both the hobbyist gold panner and the rockhound gem collector.

Information on the purchase of the Gold Panning Kit can be found on the Order Blank at the end of this book.

Wet Panning

Wet panning in water will always follow these general procedures:

— Place material suspected of containing gold in your gold pan.

— Place under sufficient water to cover operation — always — or keep pan filled with enough water to cover all material;

— Run hands through material to thoroughly wet all of it and produce a "liquid" state of suspension;

— Rotate the pan under water vigorously in a circular (or similar) motion;

— Remove larger rocks that are washed clean;

— Shake in circular motion, sideways, front to back, up or down (it all achieves the same result);

— Let lighter material "spill" off gradually.

Finally, there is only the heavier material (gold and concentrates) left in the bottom.

Crudely put? Yes. Simple? Yes. This has been going on for many thousands of years with improved expertise and improved containers (pans or vessels) making it easier. Regardless of whether I or anyone else outlines detailed instructions to save you time and effort, you will have to follow the basic procedures given above.

Dry Panning

Dry washing. or dry panning, will also follow a basic set of procedures. For example, place a blanket on the ground and shovel dry material suspected of containing gold onto it. Two people then grasp the ends of the blanket firmly and proceed to "pull" the blanket back and forth between them. The heavier particles of gold will settle through the debris and come to rest on the blanket. Pick off the top material and carry home the heavier concentrates for wet washing and further examination.

A pan is handled with the same basic procedure. Shake firmly, pick and gradually spill off the lighter material and you have saved the heavier concentrates for later classification.

Gravity Makes It Possible

Regardless of the explicit instructions you follow involving wet panning or dry washing, the weight of the heavier gold will always produce these end results. Speed may be gained by use of specialized pans and dry washers, and better results may be obtained by following specific panning procedures, but

Note the right-angle "traps" that are designed to capture gold in the Gravity Trap gold pan being demonstrated by its inventor Roy Lagal.

the reason why it all happens remains the same. Gravity forces the heavier gold and other precious metals to the bottom of any vessel or container, the same as gravity forces these heavier elements to the bottom of the river beds.

Whether gold is found in profitable quantities or not, the pleasure of sitting at the edge of mountain stream or in a long-forgotten dry gulch is one that should not be overlooked. Meanwhile, the panner is seeking to produce income with two bare hands, knowing full well that the chance always exists of hitting *the big one.*

Since Gravity Trap pans can be used for both wet and dry panning, even old stream beds and washes can be made to produce gold. Built-in riffle traps can be depended upon to trap gold whether water is present or not. True, dry panning is more difficult than wet panning and requires more practice. It can occasionally be more profitable, however, because dry streams that have not seen water for many years — or centuries — can sometimes be especially productive. They were probably passed by during the busier gold rush days!

Remember that old timers with less efficient metal pans, were almost forced to work with running water because panning there was so much easier. You may be the first person ever to pan for gold in *that* specific dry location. This fact alone can make a trip to the gold fields worthwhile.

Today's improved pans are discovering new gold producing areas daily, and the known producing areas of the past are giving up gold deposits that the old timers overlooked. Fun, excitement and profit of recreational mining are waiting in beautiful gold country. Treasure hunters of today are limited only by desire and time.

Searching for gold with pan or detector can be a truly glorious hobby because of the opportunity it affords to enjoy some of America's most beautiful country.

Hunting for Rocks

Without question, the most important and useful tool of the rockhound (besides his faithful rockhammer and patience) is a metal detector. Properly used, it can be very rewarding, but it should not be used as the ultimate answer to the positive identification of all minerals and gems. Nothing will ever replace the knowledge gained from field experience in the identification of semi-precious stones and gems. The metal detector should be used as an added accessory to the rockhound's field equipment. It will aid in the location of many conductive metallic specimens that the human eye cannot distinguish or identify.

There are many high grade specimens of different ores that can be overlooked on any given field trip. While the human eye cannot see inside an ore specimen, a good quality metal detector can.

For identification purposes the metal detector defines "metal" as any metallic substance of a conductive nature in sufficient quantity to disturb the electromagnetic field of the searchcoil. Gold, silver, copper and all the non-ferrous metals are just that – metals.

Speaking of *mineral,* we identify only those minerals that will respond to a metal detector. This is magnetic iron and iron oxide (the proper chemical content is Fe3 04.

What it all boils down to is that if a target responds as metal to a metal detector, it should be retained for further examination because it contains conductive metal in some form – and, conductive metal quite often proves valuable. A target responding as *mineral* simply contains more mineral than it does metal in any detectable form that would react to the detector. This means that for a few minutes' work you might come up with a high grade metallic sample that has been passed over for years by your fellow rockhounds.

The very low frequency of the modern detector's circuitry penetrates rocks easily and produces excellent results in identification of metallic ores. To identify metal vs. mineral specimens, use the Discriminate mode of your detector rather than its All Metal mode. Set your discrimination control at zero after you have made certain that the detector has been calibrated at the factory to reject *no* metals at that setting. You can now reject the specimens containing a high content of magnetite. Then, you may advance the discrimination setting slowly, just as you learned to do in bench testing to determine the content of the specimen and whether it is ferrous pyrite or a non-ferrous precious metal, such as gold, copper or silver.

Conduct thorough bench tests to familiarize yourself with the responses produced by both metal and mineral. Use specimens with which you are already familiar since this will greatly aid in future identification. Refer to the bench tests conducted for the identification of ore samples. Basically, they will be the same. When conducting your field search, use the detector as an *aid*, not a complete searching tool. In other words, test any likely appearing rocks. This kind of testing and investigation will greatly increase your knowledge, and just may produce for you that valuable specimen we all desire. When bench testing, always conduct each test in exactly the same manner. And, remember to test your specimen by moving it across your searchcoil at a distance of approximately one to two inches.

No matter how proficient you or an associate has proved him or herself as a rockhound, do not dismiss lightly the capabilities of a modern computerized metal detector. Just a small amount of some of the precious metals it will detect can be worth a considerable amount of money.

Let me tell you about an experience my friend Roy Lagal had at a rock and gem show. On display there were specimens from a famed gold mine. Because of its fame, these "worthless" specimens retrieved from the mine's dump were being sold for $3. It took Roy only a scan or two with a metal detector to determine that most of the specimens were metal.

He suggested to the individual with this display that some of the specimens might contain gold, but was given a polite "brush-off" and told how metal detectors were designed to find coins, not work with mine specimens. Because Roy is gentle and not an argumentative person, he simply purchased all of the slabs that had tested metallic. Some of these $3 samples were later sawed into slabs and sold to a jewelry maker for $125 per slab.

With a metal detector it was a simple matter for him to pick up these samples just loaded with precious metal!

Hunting for Bottles

Old bottles are literally *everywhere* – and they can be found by the billions! Except for occasional eye appeal or other fascination, most of these bottles are essentially worthless. There are those collectors who prize bottles, however. For them, some bottles are truly priceless. Thus, all THers are urged to be aware of the potential value of old bottles. Believe me; you're going to find them! I simply urge that you not try to ignore them.

You may not have thought of collecting bottles as a likely hobby for the THer. Still, there's a fascination and charm about searching for and finding old bottles that exists in no other field of THing. They make handsome and charming displays. Their literally limitless variety of shapes, colors and designs enable collectors to fill shelf after shelf with striking arrays.

Finally, there is real profit to be found in bottle collecting. Many bottles will command decent prices at all times, with certain specimens increasing dramatically in value as the years pass.

Acquaint yourself adequately with this widespread hobby of bottle collecting. Believe me when I tell you that as a THer you will certainly be afforded the opportunity to collect them...time and time again. When you hunt off the beaten path – with or without a metal detector – you may not always find coins, jewelry, gold nuggets or what other targets you may be seeking. But, you *will* find bottles. Yes, you can depend upon always finding bottles.

The hobby of bottle collecting goes hand in hand with any kind of THing. Valuable antique bottles can particularly be found in conjunction with relics in ghost towns and at old dump grounds. When searching for any kind of treasure, do not overlook valuable antique bottles...whether you prize them for their appearance or for a monetary value which can sometimes prove surprising. Never disparage these discoveries. They can result in a beautiful collection for you and your family, and they can also result in monetary rewards.

The search for antique bottles – collecting them and then presenting these artistic objects in colorful and creative displays – long predates the invention of even the earliest metal detector. Collecting bottles is a hobby that stretches back into antiquity. Yet, bottles remain an attractive target sought avidly today by many THers.

How can you tell a valuable bottle? Scan the various treasure, collectible and diver magazines occasionally for displays of bottles and their values. Learn to look for the different and the unusual. Have some idea of what bottles are valuable and which are just "pretty."

But, why not bring home those bottles you find that are just "pretty?" You'll develop a beautiful collection for yourself, and you'll probably find that you've retained some that are valuable as well.

Why does man search for bottles? Why has he been doing so since the very dawn of time? First, it was strictly for practical reasons. Bottles weren't attractive, In fact, they were crude and clumsy containers, scarcely more than utilitarian, not worth taking a second look at for any esthetic reason. But, they were seldom discarded because, no matter what their age, bottles could be quickly put to use for transporting and storing other materials. Then, as beauty became a more integral part of the glassmaker's art, bottles themselves evolved into objects to admire and to value.

Even though values, as measured by cash transactions, rise and fall like that of all collectibles, continually improving prices have been paid over the years for bottles...especially those that are old, oddly made or prove attractive or unusual in some other way.

The practice of bottle-making can be traced back thousands of years. Early glass manufacture was slow, costly and required hard work. Tiny jugs, jars and cosmetic cases were crudely fashioned and were prized by the ruling classes. Those who could afford these early glass containers considered them as precious as jewels. Merchants soon realized that such liquid commodities as wines, honey and oils could be stored and carried more easily in glass containers than in wood or clay.

It was not until about the time of Christ, however, that man learned to blow glass. The resulting bottles were the first of those carefully shaped, beautifully colored, hand blown objects that are so prized today by collectors.

In the twenty centuries that have since passed, literally billions of bottles have been manufactured, first by hand and later by machine. These vessels were initially designed to package primarily food and beverages, but in later centuries they became just as important to transport and present for sale medicines, cosmetics and chemicals. In earlier days, reuse of bottles was quite common. But, even then, many were discarded upon being emptied...others were discarded, either accidentally or intentionally, while still partially filled.

Few of today's bottles are reused; once emptied, they are usually quickly discarded. Of this great multitude of bottles that are thrown away daily, some are recycled; most are processed by commercial waste disposal plants and destroyed. Some few, however, will somehow find their way to join those of months, years and centuries gone by and lie by roadsides, in stream beds, in dumps and wherever mankind has left its debris. Given the beauty of many bottles and the unique nature of others, is it any wonder that collectors have come to admire and treasure them?

Obviously, then, there are literally limitless numbers of bottles to be found. The key to successful bottle hunting and collecting lies in research which is so important to all phases of THing. Good, productive locations must be found, and more of these can be located than can be searched effectively in the lifetime of any bottle hunter.

Bottles can be found today anywhere people once lived or congregated. With just a little study of history these productive sites can be located. Where were the towns, military forts, waterfronts, bridges, fords and mills once located? Where were the sites of yesterday's commerce and industry? Old newspapers, maps, historical accounts and other sources will answer all of these questions and more.

Plan to find many of your bottles associated with the water. Perhaps this is because bottles are less likely to become broken after they have been thrown into a stream or body of water. Of course, bottles protected by water are not exposed to deteriorating effects of wind and air. So, always keep your eyes open for the possibility of valuable antique bottles when you are searching in a stream, lake or any other body of water.

Some bottles survive better in water than others. When bottles are lost in the water, they become covered with sand, entrapped in sediment or – in the ocean – encrusted with reef organisms. You'll find bottles that are badly corroded while others show only mild film residue. Some will become pitted while others develop a heavy encrustation.

The laws of physics often provide real surprises for bottle hunters. Imagine, looking into a stream and discovering lying atop its bed of sand a bottle that was tossed there 100 years ago? How did this happen? You know that in a century a coin would have sunk into the earth, perhaps even below a detector's capability to detect it. How did this bottle remain on the surface? Or, has it just been somehow dug up and tossed to the surface?

Specific gravity and size and shape have a lot to do with the depth at which bottles can be found. The specific gravity or weight of any object compared with that of its surrounding materials govern the pull of the earth's gravitational field on that object. Because gold and other precious metals are heavier than the earth surrounding them, they tend to sink at every opportunity. This occurs even faster in water, where wave and wind motions often loosen bottom materials, allowing heavier objects to sink.

Since bottles are made of various earth materials such as sand and clay, their specific gravity can be the same as the river bottom sand and mud. Gravitational pull upon such manmade objects is the same as that upon surrounding materials. Thus, bottles sometimes do not sink but truly "float" on a sea of similar-weight sand, clay and gravel.

The result is a 100-year-old bottle appearing beneath you on the sandy bed of a stream!

Lakes can be treasure storehouses of bottles — of all shapes and sizes. Just because you cannot see them at first glance does not mean they are not there and have not worked their way out into deeper water. They will sink into mud and silt where you can recover them with just a little digging. Be careful, however, not to expose bare hands to fishhooks, lures, wire and other sharp objects that will also be buried in the silt.

Near the oceans where rivers rise and fall with ocean tides you can have your best success in finding bottles during times of low tides. Watch for bottle shards, broken china and other debris. In shallow waterways work around exposed boulders and sunken logs where bottles collect. Work fords, ferryboat sites and old swimming holes and under and around bridge sites. Also work downstream from these locations. At bends of rivers where the flowing water slows moving objects bottles will tend to fill and sink. Look for areas where embankments are washing away. Particularly in populated areas, these embankments will expose old bottles as they erode.

Be always on the alert for the unusual bottle, for the bottle that is different...that special bottle that attracts your attention because of its unusual nature or particularly beauty. You may have discovered a real treasure!

Staying Well

ajor benefits to be derived from treasure hunting, concern the *health* of the hobbyist – mental as well as physical! Good exercise outdoors in the fresh air... exercise that is sustained but not overly strenuous...exercise under the absolute control of the individual, if you will, benefits men and women, girls and boys, of all ages. And, the zest and thrill that the hobby brings are an absolute joy to the soul. There's no "time limit" to THing, and a hobbyist is never forced to "keep up" with a younger, more athletic or experienced competitor. Anybody can hunt for treasure for hours a day or for just a short while. The hunting may be intense or involve little exertion.

Treasure hunting is an ideal hobby for young people, full of energy and curiosity, with a restless desire to be active and discover excitement. The hobby is perhaps even more suitable for mature men and women – yes, those senior citizens, whose health permits (or *requires*) light outdoor exercise and who have maintained their zest for adventure. Adventure? Correct! What greater adventure could anyone have than finding a buried treasure...whether it be a 1¢ piece or a sack of gold coins.

People of all ages and in all physical conditions enjoy the hobby of THing. They roam parks and beaches, and they wade into the surf and swimming areas as they look for lost valuables. You'll also find hobbyists in ghost towns and in gold mining areas in search of treasure. For the most part, these people are active and dynamic. They're enthusiastic about what they are doing. And, few generally spend much time worrying about their body or their health.

Some first-time THers occasionally complain of physical aches and pains. Such complaints usually come from someone with enthusiasm who has hunted in the field all day. Of course, he or she is going to wake up next morning with sore muscles. After a short time, the soreness either disappears or is eased out of the mind by the memory of yesterday's finds. And, off they go again! Oftentimes, the discovery of another good prize proves to a better dose of medicine than any salve or liniment!

Incidentally, don't laugh at the behavior of novices. I've heard of plenty of veteran THers who go through the same experience on the first good day outside after a long winter!

I have been hunting with metal detectors for most of my adult life and have never had any serious physical problems. I develop more aches and pains from using my gym equipment. Over the years, I have developed four ways to lessen the dangers of strained or sore muscles:

• Select proper equipment, including accessories. This particularly concerns the detector's stem...if it is too long you will have a balance problem; too short, and you'll have to stoop over to search. If searchcoils are not in proper balance, the hobbyist should use an armrest or hipmount configuration.

• Strengthen hand, arm, back and shoulder muscles with a regular, planned exercise program. Not much is really required here...in fact, just using a detector will probably develop the proper muscles. At the beginning, or after a period of inactivity, however, a hobbyist should protect against strained muscles and ligaments.

• Warm-up exercises before each day's activity are generally the answer. Just a few minutes of stretching and other activity to loosen muscles and joints will prepare them for a day's work. A brisk walk, a few toe touches, a few arm and wrist curls with a one- or two-pound weight, a few body twists at the waist standing erect and perhaps a minute or two running in place...these will get the job done. You can develop your own warmup exercises.

• Finally, during metal detecting activities, use correct scanning techniques and follow accepted rules for stretching, bending and lifting. Take an occasional break. Stopping to dig a target usually provides sufficient break time. Concerning proper scanning methods, don't try to scan while balancing on one foot. Keep a firm footing and don't scan in awkward positions that may force muscles to make unnatural movements. Keep all movements as natural as possible. When scanning on steep hills, in gullies or other unlevel places, keep good balance, take shorter swings and don't place yourself in awkward positions.

Grasp the metal detector handle lightly. Slight wrist and arm movements will be necessary, but make only comfortable side-to- side swings with your searchcoil. If you must swing the coil widely, use a method that is natural and one that causes the least unnecessary wrist movements. Let the entire arm "swing," and occasionally change hands, using the other arm to manage the searchcoil.

Whenever you feel yourself tightening up, stop and rest. Most likely, however, stopping to dig targets will provide the rest you need. Actually, you should think of your next detected target as a blessing. You'll get to stop, stoop down and dig the target. This activity gives other muscles a workout, which will help prevent sore muscles that come from long periods of continuous searchcoil swinging without a break.

Most important of all, use common sense and take care of yourself! There are no "time limits" to metal detecting. You have the rest of your life.

When to Hunt

And, speaking of time...You may be asking...just when should I hunt? Is there a special time better than others? Time of day? Time of year?

The answer to all your questions is to hunt any time...day or night, morning or evening, rain or shine, summer or winter...all seasons are THing seasons. Use your own best judgment and, always remember, you're hunting because you *want to* and because you *enjoy it*. If the hobby should ever become tedious or boring, give it a rest and wait for your interest to return. Frankly, I can't imagine that hunting for treasure could ever be boring, what with all the wonderful coins, items of jewelry and other valuable objects just waiting to be found.

But, when to hunt...here are some suggestions. After your evening meal, you might go to a nearby park or swimming area to search for an hour or so. On weekends you can spend as much of the days as you like searching outlying and out-of-town sites. On vacations make it a habit to stop along the roadway at various parks and roadside stops where you and your family can stretch your legs and refresh yourselves. At the same time, you can search and recover a coin or two lost by those folks who have used the park before you.

Treasure hunting is a good way to limber up in the morning and get the blood circulating. Get up an hour earlier than normal; drive to the park or into any public area and search along heavily congested traffic paths. Get out before most people do; the rewards will be yours. If you work in an area close to a park or any location where people play or congregate, you can walk over to this area during your lunch break and hunt for half an hour or so. Any time you're driving along and see an area that looks promising...stop, get out with your detector and scan a sweep or two. You'll never know what you may find until your detector sings out and you dig!

Physical Dangers

These probably won't ever happen but if you're in the wrong place at the right time, there's always the chance of your being attacked by hoodlums or drunks. If you lack confidence in the security of an area, work in pairs. Some THers carry a can of "mace" or similar deterrent, not stored away in a bag but where it is readily accessible to them. I suggest you never tell anyone, even children, the amount of

Treasure hunting can be a glorious hobby indeed, offering enjoyment and excitement, exercise and fresh air...plus the prospect of finding hidden wealth.

treasure you are finding. The quickest way to discourage people is to show them a few pulltabs and bottlecaps. They'll suddenly lose interest and even the children won't be so anxious to help you dig. Never tell inquisitive people how much your detector is worth. Just say, "Oh, they don't cost very much; besides, this detector was a gift." In fact, it probably was a gift, either from yourself or from your spouse.

There's the danger too of being bothered by animals. Often when I jog or work in unfamiliar areas, I wear a four-foot length of chain around my waist. A quick-release clip attached to one end makes a neat fastener. Only a mighty strong-willed animal will stay around after one blow from my weapon. I'm glad, though, that I've never had to use it.

Always be alert to the possibility of digging up explosives. Over the past half century some areas have been used from time to time as bombing and artillery ranges. Now, these areas are certainly few and far between. Nevertheless, if you dig up a strange-looking device that you suspect might be a bomb or artillery shell, notify the authorities immediately. Let them take care of it. Then exercise caution when digging in that area, or just stay away entirely.

Watch where you're walking! Of course, you won't fall in the holes you dig, certainly, but joggers and others might, if you fail to cover them. So...*fill your holes!*

Many natural sites represent a fragile environment that can be easily damaged or destroyed. Please leave only footprints — not pulltabs, wrappers, cans or other souvenirs of our "disposable" civilization. Remember, a fellow treasure hunter may want to work the area someday. *You may even want to come back yourself!*

These adventurers seeking gold veins in an abandoned mine must exercise safety precautions that are not required for everyday THers.

When campfires are covered and not doused with water, coals remain very hot even till the next day and can cause severe burns. Watch out for coals, even when they appear cold.

Toxic waste presents an increasingly serious problem. Be alert to any area (or any piece of flotsam or jetsam) that looks or smells bad...in any way. *Keep away from anything* that you suspect of being contaminated .

Don't Get Stung!

The above warning doesn't concern buying a low quality detector...that's discussed elsewhere in this book! It's inevitable that people who venture into the out-of-doors are going to encounter gnats, mosquitoes, bees, ants, wasps, spiders, ticks, hornets, scorpions or other such creatures. You don't need to be told to try to avoid them. Even when you can't, however, all that usually results is a brief moment or so of slight discomfort or pain. But, the results can be deadly.

Since the THer is out of doors, he should be aware of the dangers from insects and other varmints. Of course, the greatest danger from most of these is during the warm months of late spring, summer and early fall. There is very little danger during cold weather. To avoid insects, generally, it's good idea not to use scented preparations such as deodorants, hair spray and perfume which might tend to attract them. If you're in an unknown area or one where you've been bothered by insects before, keep a can of insecticide handy.

If you are allergic to stings, follow your doctor's advice. The bite of a spider can be very dangerous, and that of a scorpion will be very painful. So, be especially alert for them. You're most likely to find spiders around old buildings, old lumber, dump grounds and trash areas. They might also be in old houses or areas that have not been disturbed for some time. Scorpions can be found in warmer climates. To avoid spiders, scorpions and similar creatures, always be careful where you put your hands and feet. It's been 20 years since I've even seen a scorpion, so you have little to fear if you just watch your step and where you place your hands.

Use good common sense. Wear sturdy gloves when moving debris and lumber. Look on the underside of lumber and other large objects before picking it up, whenever possible. Don't get under old buildings or porches unless you proceed cautiously. You might want to consider wearing a hat or scarf to keep insects out of your hair, especially when searching in or under an old structure. Always carefully inspect any areas before you enter them. Ticks and chiggers (in Texas, for sure!) give some of us real fits. Their season starts in March or April and ends in September, with the peak coming in the hottest months. Of course, fire ants in many places seem to have devoured most ticks, but it seems ants are now more of a problem than ticks used to be!

I'm certainly not trying to scare you with all this talk about insects and such. But, it's a good idea to keep them in mind any time you're out of doors.

Actually, from the standpoint of health and safety the worst things that will probably ever befall a THing hobbyist are sunburn and getting wet in a sudden storm. Even these can be minimized by sunscreen, proper clothing and following common sense rules of exposure.

Above all, use your use your good common sense, and you'll be fine! Don't let needless worry interfere with the joy and thrill of THing. Accurate knowledge will not only help you dispel any unreasonable fears, but materially reduce the chances of encountering problems. It is the *unknown* that we fear most.

Remember the Boy Scout motto: Be Prepared.

THing and the Law

This chapter is by no means intended to offer legal advice. In fact, I've always believed that the best advice you can give anyone who wonders about having a legal problem is, "See a lawyer." This chapter, instead, will seek to raise just a few legal points that you should consider before going out into the field to hunt for treasure and to remind you that there are laws applicable to various treasure hunting situations. Each state has its own laws concerning where you can hunt for treasure and whether you may keep treasure when it is found. You should learn these laws.

All states have laws against trespassing. If a sign says, "Keep Out," do just that. It is always best to seek permission. Anyway, how can you listen to your metal detector if you have to keep an ear cocked for a returning property owner...or, a siren?

With the proper attitude and a true explanation of your purpose, you will be surprised at the cooperation you will receive from most landowners. The majority of them will be curious enough about your metal detector and what you hope to find, to agree to let you search. Offer to split, giving them 25% (or less) of all you find and they will usually be more willing. If large amounts of treasure are believed to be hidden or buried on another's property, a properly drawn legal agreement is a *must!* Such an agreement between both you and all landowners (husband and wife, etc.) will eliminate any later disagreements which might otherwise arise.

Here's a suggestion on how to help *prove* that you're a professional treasure hunter. Have some cards printed. Yes, that's right...business cards with your name address and telephone number that advertise your services with a metal detector to help find lost items. Pass these cards out as you travel and give quantities to local jewelers and insurance agents. Place the cards on bulletin boards in appropriate places.

Ownership of Property

Finder's Keepers — There may be some truth in this old statement, especially about unmarked items such as coins. But, there are certainly exceptions, particularly when you start considering other objects whose ownership can be more easily identified. No matter what kind of treasure you are looking for, I urge you to have a general knowledge of the laws of ownership. You can never tell what you'll find or where you'll find it! Finder's Keepers may not be appropriate for an object you discover on private or posted property if the landowner decides to dispute your claim. On the other hand, Finder's Keepers generally applies to any owner-not-identified item you find when you are not trespassing, when you are hunting legally on any public land and when the rightful owner cannot be identified. Of course, anyone can claim ownership of anything you find; it may then be left to the courts to decide the rightful owner.

Treasure trove — In the United States this is broadly defined as any gold or silver in coin, plate or bullion and paper currency that has been found concealed in the earth or in a house belonging to another person, even when found hidden in movable property belonging to others such as a book, bureau, safe or a piece of machinery. To be classed as treasure trove the item(s) must have been lost long enough to indicate that the original owner is dead or unknown. All found property can generally be separated into five legal categories:

Abandoned property, as a general rule, is a tangible asset discarded or abandoned willfully and intentionally by its original owners. Thus, it becomes the property of the first person who discovers and desires it. An example would be a household item such as an appliance discarded into a trash receptacle. If the trash collector (or anyone else, for that matter) decides to take the appliance, they can do so legally.

210

Concealed property is tangible property hidden by its owners to prevent observation, inventory, acquisition or possession by other parties. In most cases, when such property is found, the courts order its return to the original owner. Sometimes the finder is given a small reward, more for his honesty in reporting the find than for the effort of discovery.

Lost property is defined as that which the owner has inadvertently and unintentionally lost, yet to which he legally retains title. Still, there is a presumption of abandonment until the owner appears and claims such property, providing that the finder has taken steps to notify the owner of its discovery. Such a case might arise when someone finds a lost wallet that contains documents identifying the owner. It is the general rule that such property must be returned to its owner, who pays a reward if he so desires In fact, in almost every jurisdiction a criminal statute exists that makes it a crime to withhold "lost" property.

Misplaced property has been intentionally hidden or laid away by its owner who planned to retrieve it at a later date but forgot about the property or where it was hidden. When found, such property is generally treated the same as concealed property with attempts required to find its owner. When this is not possible, ownership usually reverts to the occupant or owner of the premises on which it was found with the finder being awarded some amount of the object's value.

Things embedded in the soil generally constitute property other than treasure trove, such as antique bottles or artifacts of historical value. The finder acquires no rights to the object, and possession of such objects belongs to the landowner unless declared otherwise by a court of law. Generally, courts divide the value of the find between the property owner and the finder.

Rules of Conduct

Of course, the first rule of conduct for any treasure hunter is to *fill all holes*. You'll learn that most every governmental subdivision — be it city, township, county, state or whatever — enforces some sort of law that prohibits destruction of public or private property. When you dig a hole or cut through the grass on private or public property, you're in effect violating a law. Of course, laws are generally not enforced this rigidly, especially if the THer is careful in his digging and retrieving.

In addition, property should always be restored to the condition in which you found it. I have heard of treasure hunters who completely devastate an area, leaving large gaping holes, tearing down structures and uprooting shrubbery and sidewalks. Damage of this kind is one of the reasons we're seeing so many efforts at legislation that would literally *shut down* metal detectors on public property.

Of course, there have always been laws to protect private as well as public property, but only in recent years have these been rigidly enforced to limit the activity of metal detector hobbyists. Why has this happened? Public lands, parks, recreational areas and such are continuously maintained and kept in good condition so that those using such facilities can enjoy them to the fullest. When there is wilful destruction, laws protecting the property are more rigidly enforced and new laws are sought. There are numerous methods you can use to retrieve coins and other objects without destroying landscaping and making unsightly messes.

An experienced THer seeks to leave an area that has been searched in such a condition that nobody will know that it has ever been searched. I always urge hobbyists to leave any area they search in *better* condition than they found it! All treasure hunters must become aware of their responsibility to protect the property of others and to keep public property fit for all. Persons who destroy property, leave large holes unfilled, or tear down buildings in search of valuables, should not to be called treasure hunters — but, more properly...looters and scavengers.

Taxes

All treasure that you find must be declared as income during the year in which you receive a monetary gain from that treasure. If you find $1,000 in coins, which you spend at once because they have no numismatic value, then you must

212

declare the face value of those coins in the current year's income tax report. If, however, you discover a valuable coin — or, say, an antique pistol — you do not make a declaration until you sell the item(s) and then only for the amount you received. If you decide to donate some of your finds to historical societies or museums, you may be able to deduct the fair market price of the items as charitable contributions. Simply stated, the tax laws require you to declare all income from treasure hunting.

You may be allowed to deduct some or all of your expenses but you must have good records. You are advised to check with a tax accountant, especially if you plan to become a full-time treasure hunter. An accountant will advise you as to what type records you are required to keep.

Code of Ethics

Filling holes and protecting the landscaping is but one requirement of a dedicated metal detector hobbyist. Thousands of individuals and organization have adopted a formal Metal Detector Operators Code of Ethics:

"— I will respect private and public property, all historical and archaeological sites and will do no metal detecting on these lands without proper permission.

"— I will keep informed on and obey all laws, regulations and rules governing federal, state and local public lands.

"— I will aid law enforcement officials whenever possible.

"— I will cause no willful damage to property of any kind, including fences, signs and buildings, and will always fill holes I dig.

"— I will not destroy property, buildings or the remains of ghost towns and other deserted structures.

"— I will not leave litter or uncovered items lying around. I will carry all trash and dug targets with me when I leave each search area.

"— I will observe the Golden Rule, using good outdoor manners and conducting myself at all times in a manner that will add to the stature and public image of all people engaged in the field of metal detection."

Policing this code is an important job of the scores of local metal detector and treasure hunting clubs organized over the nation. Clubs varying in size from a few members to hundreds meet regularly for fellowship, to share adventures and to compare their success in the field and water. At the same time, these sincere hobbyists seek knowledge of new developments in the science of metal detecting and try to remain abreast of the rapidly changing laws and regulations that govern their hobby. I believe that almost every hobbyist — especially one just learning about metal detectors — can benefit from membership in a club.

The hobby and sport of metal detecting has been kept clean and dignified by people who care about their hobby, themselves and their fellow men. Most detector owners go out of their way to protect a most rewarding and enjoyable hobby and to share their enjoyment with others. Keeping the hobby clean takes the effort and dedication of everyone...not just a few. So, as you go about enjoying your leisure, or perhaps full-time activity, be professional! Be worthy of your calling!

I wish you success and happiness and maybe...

I'll see you in the field!

21 – Technology Has Improved Them...

More on Detectors

M etal detectors designed primarily for treasure hunting come in a wide range of sizes and shapes. This closing chapter is designed to tell you a little more about them with emphasis on the three basic types — computerized, motion and non-motion.

Detectors can vary in price by hundreds of dollars with some models sold very inexpensively. Pay $79.95 for a "cheap" detector, however, and you'll probably have difficulty locating a penny lying on a vinyl floor.

This *Treasure Hunting Text*, therefore, has been concerned only with modern and "capable" detectors...those designed and manufactured with quality and, thus, having the ability to find treasure.

As I have helped develop metal detectors over the past three decades, circuitry to transmit and receive signals has improved progressively year by year. Many of my old detectors, though obviously obsolete today, are still in use and can find treasure. I do not intend to discuss *obsolete* instruments, however; a newcomer to the hobby has no business trying to hunt with any of them. If you're buying your first detector, I implore you to start out with a modern instrument.

Because detectors with Very Low Frequency (VLF) circuitry are far and away today's most popular, they are the only type that this chapter will discuss. The VLF name comes from the operation of this detector in the Very Low (radio) Frequency spectrum of 3 to 30 kilohertz. Most VLF detectors operate no higher than about 15kHz with the majority operating near 5kHz.

Computerized Detectors

My career in metal detection has extended over some 30 years. I can state categorically, however, that the technology of metal detection has changed (improved) more in the past half-dozen years than during the preceding 25. The reason? In a word...microprocessors.

The finest metal detectors available today – and, in the foreseeable future – are instruments with computerized circuitry based on microprocessor controls such as those in Garrett's CX and Ultra GTA series. At the time of this book's publication, Garrett had just begun volume manufacturing of its fifth such instrument, the Grand Master Hunter CX III with revolutionary new *TreasureTalk*™. Our Company also manufactures the Grand Master Hunter CX II, the Master Hunter CX, the Ultra GTA 1000 and the GTA 500, all of which utilize computerized circuitry with microprocessor controls. I know that they are without a doubt *the finest metal detectors ever manufactured*.

They have proved themselves to me and to countless others who have found treasure with them. They are so simple to operate that even novices are pushing a single touchpad and finding treasure immediately. This is not to say that other Garrett detectors are not outstanding instruments that represent real value for the THer. And, there are other manufacturers who produce capable detectors, although I would not feel particularly comfortable in commenting on them.

It is well to understand that only those instruments employing a microprocessor as the integral control element can be considered computerized detectors...or, can be expected to give the performance that a THer should expect from a computerized instrument.

Unfortunately, some who either make or sell detectors have confused the issue by abusing the term *computer* in advertising and promotional materials. Such terms as "computer-aided," "computer-enhanced" and "computer-designed" have been used to describe detectors. To the best

216

of my knowledge *none of these so-described detectors utilizes microprocessor controls.* Perhaps some of their circuit designs were improved by use of a computer. (I know that those of all Garrett detectors were.) Perhaps target responses were tested by a computer program. Perhaps a computer was used in some way to manufacture the detector. (We use computers in our manufacturing processes at Garrett.)

Still, to qualify as a real computerized detector *in the field,* the only place that counts for a true THer, an instrument **must** incorporate microprocessors in its circuitry.

Simply stated, the computerized detector is a *thinking machine;* it performs literally millions of analytical computations almost simultaneously to make circuitry adjustments that were formerly made by hand by the hobbyist. As the searchcoil receives data, it is fed into microprocessor circuitry in digital form and instantaneously compared with the "mind" of the computer — i.e., data that has been stored in the computer at the factory. Thus, knowledge that formerly was required from the operator is now contained within the computer, which results in automatic adjustments that once required manual action. Not only does the computerized detector make these adjustments automatically, but they are made at once...when they are needed, not when an operator finally notices (or, remembers) the them...if, indeed, the operator even understands that they are needed.

As the detector is scanned, it continually performs self-tests; that is, it self-adjusts to achieve optimum operating performance for all conditions, including battery condition, temperature changes, ground mineral variations and even the possible aging of electronic components that might cause "values" to change. Target data coming through the detector's searchcoil is compared with the particular requirements that can be selected by the operator (such as discrimination) to produce the proper audio and meter indications. False signals caused by conventional detector "back reading" are eliminated. Even large objects are properly read on the meter with the precise audio tone given.

Let me emphasize, however, that our new Garrett CX and Ultra GTA detectors are "single-touch" instruments. No adjustments in any controls need ever be made unless the operator specifically desires them. Yet, each of these detectors is designed to begin finding treasure after only one touchpad has been pressed.

Garrett engineers have known for years that dissimilar ground mineral conditions cause different discriminating performance. The Grand Master Hunter CX II and III, thus. have various scanning methods stored in their memory banks. As earth mineralization changes while either of these instruments is being scanned, the detector automatically readjusts itself to use the optimum discrimination method. Additionally, every Garrett computerized detector automatically monitors every atmospheric and ground condition to maintain circuitry at optimum levels.

Garrett's computerized instruments permit the ultimate in THing. No better detectors have ever been devised for the hobby. Greater depth and considerably more discriminating accuracy is possible. Of course, just as some capabilities that can be achieved with computerized microprocessor-controlled detectors aren't possible with conventional instruments, the capabilities may not be required by all THers.

But, it has been said that operator "mistakes" can be virtually eliminated with the "thinking" detectors. I know of treasures discovered all over the world that could never have been found before. "Worked-out" areas are producing vast amounts of new discoveries of coins and jewelry. Because these new finds are ones that were buried more deeply or were masked by trash, they are usually older and more valuable than objects previously found in the same areas.

Computerized detectors permit professional performance and detection accuracy to be achieved easily by beginners at levels that have tantalized professionals for years. We have truly entered the era of hi-tech metal detector performance. Treasure hunting and all other forms of metal detecting will never be the same again!

Garrett Development

Garrett's computerized and microprocessor-controlled instruments are the products of more than 10 years of intensive research and study in the application of microprocessor technology to the field of metal detection. Along with this analytical investigation came the necessary laboratory and field tests to produce what are truly the world's first *thinking* metal detectors.

In one sense, they are not *new* metal detectors, since the capabilities of each are built upon 30-plus years spent by Garrett Electronics in developing technology and expertise...all this in addition to my experience gained in the parks, woods and waters of the world along with that faithfully reported to us by countless thousands of hobbyists who have used Garrett instruments to find treasure.

In a real sense, however, the computerized instruments are *absolutely new* and revolutionary detectors. They utilize the very latest in microprocessor technology...expertise that has never been brought to any metal detection instrument before.

Garrett engineers began working in the mid-70s on the first U. S. patent for computerized circuitry based on microprocessor control of a metal detector (#4,709,213). Because we recognized that a detector had to be *easy to use* if it was to be successful, roughly a decade passed before this technology was included in a Garrett detector. We recognized that a hobbyist wants to spend time looking for treasure...not programming a detector!

The first Grand Master Hunter was developed because we at Garrett have never been satisfied with any detector that we ever manufactured. *We always sought to do better!* It has been our continuing goal, year by year, to update and improve the quality, performance and capabilities – in short, the *value* – of each piece of equipment that is sold bearing the Garrett trademark and, thus, representing the Garrett tradition of excellence.

We had long recognized the feasibility of using microprocessor chips in the circuitry of a metal detector to improve its capabilities with computerized technology. When ultra-low-power microprocessor technology made such chips available for metal detectors, we realized that the time had come to complete our design, then to manufacture and market this computerized detector.

Stringent Testing

It is well known in metal detecting – indeed, in any design endeavor – that extensive laboratory and field testing are essential for success. In fact, for the development of field-worthy, high performance equipment, it is necessary that the amount of testing in the field – in hours, certainly – exceed that done in the laboratory. It is simply impossible to manufacture equipment that will perform at maximum levels under actual outdoor conditions unless countless weeks and months are spent in the field testing such equipment.

A continual process of building prototypes, testing them, building new models, testing them, continuing to improve designs, etc. must be carried out. In fact, it's a *never-ending* process! And, for a detector to respond fully to all demands, such testing must be conducted in various locations over the world in addition to the United States.

This is the testing and development program of Garrett Electronics. The author, his field engineers, employee hobbyists and other veteran THers and electronic prospectors

Facing
Long ago Charles Garrett vowed to "practice what I preach," which means rigorously testing any Garrett detector before it is ever offered to the public.

Over
Note touchpads and Graphic Target Analyzers on control panels of Grand Master Hunter CX III, above, and Ultra GTA 1000, lower right, and GTA 500.

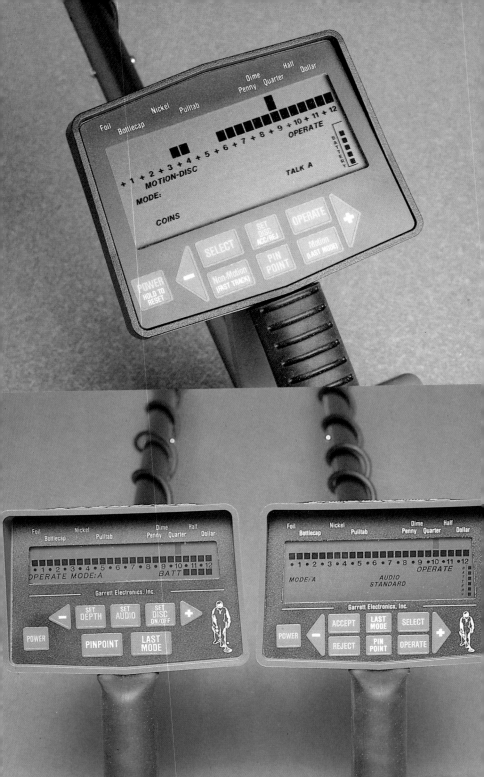

spend countless hours over many months and years testing all types of new equipment. Indeed, because of this testing, some new detectors are never offered to the public. All equipment is actually used under field conditions over ground mineral areas ranging from zero to absolute maximum mineralization. Every detector is subjected to rugged environmental tests.

Results from three decades of operations speak for themselves. Garrett Electronics would never consider producing — much less, trying to market — any equipment today without complete initial field testing and thorough analysis of all prior test data, followed by extensive test programs in actual THing locations as the new equipment is developed. Such extensive testing at all levels is one of the reasons why the new computerized detectors exceed all other metal detectors available today in capabilities and in rugged, reliable performance.

Microprocessor technology gave us the capability to build equipment utilizing super low-power circuitry with extremely low signal-to-noise ratios and fantastic gains. This technology, therefore, offered the capability of *pre-analyzing* the soil and all detected targets which would never have been possible with existing circuitry. It became readily apparent that the amount of data we were receiving from existing searchcoils through existing circuits — while the best in the detector industry — was woefully inferior to that available through the technology of microprocessors and computers.

Facing
Computerized analysis (colors show stress levels) enables Garrett engineers to maintain light weight while designing stronger, more efficient equipment.
Over
Garrett detectors are tested under all types of conditions and in all sorts of soils such as this test plot located in highly mineralized ground.

For example, data received from a searchcoil on a particular target is called a "target signature." It contains all the data about each target that can be acquired from the electromagnetic field. Iron minerals send similar signatures.

Microprocessor technology gives us the capability to analyze within a fraction of a second — and, on a continuing basis — every bit of this signature information.

Garrett Electronics was challenged as it had never been before. Talented new personnel and expensive equipment were required for Garrett to be able to respond appropriately.

Essentially, we needed new laboratory electronic design equipment with computerized circuitry that permitted total analysis of all signature data as it was received from the ground. Such data could then be compared with that analyzed by the existing Master Hunter equipment and technology.

Because our new computer equipment was also capable of systematically analyzing all existing circuitry and printed circuit boards (PCBs), an immediate benefit to Garrett and its customers was an upgrading of circuitry and PCBs in all models. We gained the ability to vastly improve current models even without the use of a microprocessor chip.

All of Garrett's detectors were upgraded through this program. Yet, we always recognized that to utilize fully the capabilities of microprocessors in a detector, we needed to design and build an all-new instrument. And, we demanded that such a new instrument utilize the 30 years of field application and the experience in automatic ground balancing that were represented in Garrett's expertise.

The result is two new series of detectors that can operate at 100% efficiency at the push of a single touchpad. No other control adjustment is necessary. In addition, the Grand Master Hunter CX II and III offer the exclusive *Fast Track*™ and *Ground Track*™ automatic and continuous ground balancing features, and the CX also provides *Fast Track*. The two Ultra GTA detectors make exclusive notch discrimination capabilities available that are now satisfying the exacting performance requirements of the most demanding THer.

226

Furthermore, the *value* these new detectors offer is second to none. Increasing the value received for each dollar of detector investment continues as a major Garrett goal.

These revolutionary detectors give far better performance, detection depth, accuracy of detection and accuracy of target identification over all types of soil than any other instrument ever available. The Company's new CX detectors automatically analyze the soil and adjust ground balance — continually and automatically — even as they analyze all detector targets. The GTA instruments offer precise *notch* discrimination capabilities that had previously existed only in the dreams of THers.

Automatically programmed into the circuitry of each detector is a wealth of information that THers previously had to retain in their heads — or notebooks. Veteran hobbyists remember the importance of remaining continually on the alert for changing ground mineral conditions...how they had to analyze various targets and, often, conflicting discrimination signals received from a detector. Now, much of this human analytical aspect that was formerly required has been assumed by the microprocessor-controlled circuitry in these detectors. This is why we believe them truly to be "thinking" detectors. Garrett Electronics is proud to offer each of them to treasure hunters of the world!

Of course, the new Grand Master Hunter CX III also offers *TreasureTalk*, which enables the detector literally to *talk* to its operator to assist in regulating the detector and detecting targets.

Amazing, indeed!

Motion Detectors

The motion-type detector with automatic ground balance is probably the most popular model generally used today by THers. First of all, it is easy to use. Added to this are its capabilities for finding coins and jewelry that are almost equal to those of higher priced detectors. This capability becomes particularly apparent when both expensive and average-priced models are in the hands of a novice. Yet, while most models from reputable manufacturers are capable, some will definitely detect treasure deeper than others.

Primary difference between the motion and non-motion detectors is expressed by the names themselves. The motion detector must be kept moving slightly for detection to occur. But, there is another important difference. On the motion detector there can be no manually adjustable ground balance (iron mineral elimination) control. That function is performed automatically and electronically.

An important feature of motion detectors is *discrimination*. In fact, all quality modern metal detectors have circuitry and controls that allow an operator to use touchpads or dials to eliminate detection of certain classes of targets. This process, of course, is called *discrimination*.

On the older instruments the usual discrimination control was a dial that cumulatively eliminated targets based on conductivity. With various targets placed on the dial in the order of their conductivity the operator set his controls to indicate which targets the detector should accept by eliminating those with lower conductivity.

Garrett's new series of computerized Ultra GTA motion detectors features revolutionary new "notch" discrimination that offers 24 separate and distinct classes of targets, enabling an operator to set the detector so that it can isolate any one target to seek out...or any one junk metal type to ignore — regardless of the location of these targets on the conductivity scale. Any one of these 24 types of targets can be removed from detection, singularly or in any combination.

In other words, a THer can "notch" his GTA detector to hunt for only one kind of target. This has proven especially helpful to hobbyists participating in competition hunts who are looking for a token made of a special type of metal. With the GTA they can find *only* these targets.

From time to time a THer discovers quantities of specific trash targets that simply cannot be eliminated from detection by factory-set discrimination — unless valuable targets with similar conductivity are eliminated as well. On Garrett's GTA detectors the these pesky pieces of junk can be rejected easily. Just move the searchcoil across a junk target and watch the GTA's Upper Scale for its response and push the **REJECT** touchpad. No more trouble from that type of trash metal!

There are numerous reasons why a THer would want to accept or reject specific targets:

• You may be looking for *only one item*...a certain lost piece of jewelry, for example. The GTA can be programmed to reject *all other* types of metal targets.

• You may be hunting in an area where you are plagued with a specific type of trash. You can reject *just this type* of trash metal and continue to hunt for all other metal targets.

• You may have your own *special* ideas for designing a mode of detection. The Ultra GTA detectors present unlimited opportunities to try out any and all of your ideas.

Some quality detectors feature both the motion and non-motion modes. Thus, when the non-motion (or, All Metal) mode is being used, manual ground balance controls are available for adjustment to achieve precise iron mineral elimination.

Motion detectors, especially when discrimination is required, are most efficient when detecting coin-sized targets. They are not recommended for cache hunting, relic hunting and gold hunting. As you gain experience with this type detector you will learn that the detector sometimes has difficulty analyzing large and irregularly shaped targets which can cause the signals to break up or be erratic.

A technique you will especially have to practice is pinpointing, especially in manicured lawns or other areas where determining an exact location before digging is important. Since hovering over a target is not possible, manual pinpointing will be more difficult. Electronic pinpointing which is offered on all of the better models overcomes this possible deficiency.

To activate electronic pinpointing, a switch or control must be operated as described in the *Operator's Manual* for the instrument. This mode sharpens detection signals and activates a non-motion All Metal mode. The detector can then be hovered, and detection signals are sharpened. Thus, the target can be more accurately pinpointed. If even more precise pinpointing is needed, detuning (tuning to the target) can be brought into play. The operator draws an imaginary "X" on the ground, and determines the area where maximum signal occurs. The searchcoil is placed directly upon the ground. The pinpoint switch is pressed and released, momentarily, and then depressed and held. This switching action tunes the detector to the target. As the searchcoil is scanned over the target, a sharp audio sound will be heard when the target is directly below the center point of the searchcoil.

Simply stated, however, pinpointing generally presents no problem for anyone searching for coins or jewelry because such targets can be considered comparatively large. Tiny gold nuggets present a different story entirely!

Quality motion detectors rank high among all types in detection depth. Not only is it capable of detecting deep coins, but its extremely sharp and quick response signal is unmistakable when rings and other such valuable metallic objects are detected. In addition, all quality detectors will offer some form of trash elimination through discrimination control(s).

Many hobbyists find the automated motion models fairly satisfactory for types of metal detecting other than routine hunting for coins and jewelry, particularly those instruments produced by quality manufacturers. In fact, I've used our Ultra GTA models for shallow relic hunting. Some hobbyists even report finding gold nuggets with an automated instrument.

To operate one of the motion type detectors simply turn the instrument on and start scanning. No ground balancing adjustments are necessary. You can set the audio to either silent or threshold and "notch" or dial in your desired adjustments in discrimination. Always wear headphones for improved efficiency.

Scan the searchcoil in front of you in the side-to-side motion as explained in this book. Keep in mind that you cannot hover the searchcoil over a target, but I don't consider this a problem. Just scan as you normally would at a rate of about one to two feet per second, and you will get good depth of detection.

Although these detectors do not shape up for gold, cache and relic hunting, they do a superb job of finding coins, jewelry and other similar targets anywhere, and you can count on them to produce quite well in most phases of ghost towning.

If you're interested in a detector that will perform satisfactorily in situations other than primarily hunting for coins or jewelry in a park or on the beach, I suggest that you learn more about the non-motion and computerized models.

Non-Motion Detectors

This trusty type of detector — the *only* instrument that veterans will use for hunting caches or gold nuggets (or just about anything else for that matter) — is last for two reasons:

1. Only a veteran has any reason to be hunting with one of them. Everyone else should be using a motion detector, preferably a computerized GTA with notch discrimination.

2. Any veteran who *truly* desires the depth and sensitivity that is really possible only with a non-motion detector with its All Metal mode should be hunting with a computerized instrument like those discussed on the first pages of this chapter!

But, let's talk about non-motion detectors anyway. Until the development of the automated motion detector these instruments whose ground balance had to be adjusted manually dominated the treasure hunting field. They represented such an improvement over earlier detectors which had but limited (*non-existent* sometimes seemed a better description) ability to eliminate iron earth minerals and wetted salt.

Non-motion detectors could be manually adjusted to ignore the effects of iron mineralization and detect only metal targets. Quality non-motion detectors have been highly popular instruments capable of performing all THing tasks. They will produce signals continuously while hovering motionless over targets. They detect very deeply and are offered with an array of desirable features. Operating in the All Metal mode, the detector can be precisely ground balanced, but no discrimination is possible. All metallic targets will be detected.

Almost all of the better models also offer a second mode of hunting that includes motion capability in a Discriminate mode with automatic ground balance. This permits discrimination that will eliminate discovery of unwanted junk targets as announced by a sound from your detector. It is a fact of metal detector technology, however, that an instrument can always detect targets deeper when operating in a genuine non-motion All Metal mode. The trade-off, thus, becomes maximum depth that is possible in a non-motion All Metal mode, which usually requires manual ground balancing, vs. the convenience of discrimination that is possible with automatic ground balance, even though promising less depth.

Yet, the new Grand Master Hunter CX III is unique! It lets you enjoy the all the advantages of discrimination while hunting in a true non-motion All Metal mode. Here's how.

First of all, why do you really use discrimination? To keep from finding and having to dig unwanted targets, obviously! And, your detector sounds off on *all* targets when you're hunting in an All Metal mode with no discrimination! Well, the Upper Scale on the GTA of the CX III will indicate (and TreasureTalk will *tell you*) the precise conductivity of every target you find. You can compare this information with the Coin ID Guide above the scale, add in your own experience and then decide whether you want to dig or not.

We call this "LCD discrimination!" And, it's possible only with the Grand Master Hunter CX III.

Furthermore, some modern computerized detectors, such as the Grand Master Hunter CX II and III and Master Hunter CX, offer *Fast Track™* — one-touchpad automatic ground balancing — as an alternative to manual ground balancing. Plus, the CX II and III also give you *Ground Track™*, which can make the process of automatic ground balancing continuous in the non-motion All Metal mode.

In fact, ground balancing has become an aspect of metal detecting that hobbyists can truly take for granted! I believe that in just a few years all quality detectors will provide automatic ground balance. What an improvement this is...especially after all the problems that we veteran THers have experienced over the years with ground balance. Still, many of today's quality non-motion detectors, including the CX II and CX III, permit the treasure hunter to adjust ground balance manually...and there are THers who *demand* this capability for their precise hunting requirements.

Since quality non-motion detectors are so highly capable, they can be selected and used with the utmost confidence. The unescapable fact is, however, that manual adjust non-motion detectors are just a little more difficult to use than the automated motion models because they have to be ground balanced. No, let's admit it. The fact is that the non-computerized models are a *lot* more difficult to use.

At the same time, however, non-motion detectors offer more versatility and will usually provide greater satisfaction in more different areas of metal detecting. A computerized non-motion detector, therefore, can provide a valuable addition to any treasure hunting arsenal.

Of course, any of these instruments will fulfill every expectation of most coin hunters capable of mastering the ground balancing techniques. In addition, non-motion detectors can meet all requirements of those hunting for caches, relics and gold nuggets with ease and efficiency.

The non-motion detector is especially commended to the individual who has already exhibited real proficiency in hunting for coins but already has an "itch" to try out the other types of metal detecting. As noted earlier, many hobbyists use motion detectors for tasks other than hunting for coins and jewelry, but non-motion models will generally detect deeper than motion models no matter what the target!

Because of its manual controls, this detector is obviously capable of more precise ground balance than a motion detector whose automatic ground balance is regulated at the factory. Such precision will rarely be required by the average coin hunter. Not so with relic and cache hunters seeking deep targets, electronic prospectors seeking deep ore veins or nugget hunters who work over highly mineralized ground. All of these THers demand absolute ground balance that will enable them to hear faint signals from faraway or tiny targets.

Any kind of pinpointing technique is possible with non-motion detectors since they can be hovered over a target at will. Still, pinpointing is never a problem because modern, quality instruments all offer precise electronic pinpointing circuitry. In addition, the Garrett CX family of detectors all have an LCD readout or a meter that will indicate (literally *tell* you, in the case of the CX III) depth of coin-size targets.

Non-motion detectors will respond "positive" to "hot rocks," which are mineralized rocks that contain a highly concentrated magnetic iron/conductive element content differing from the matrix to which the detector has been ground balanced. Hot rock response is troublesome in some areas, but the non-motion detector will not indicate its presence unless the hot rock is close to the searchcoil, a maximum distance roughly equal to the diameter of the searchcoil.

Be certain discrimination controls are set to "zero" when you're testing hot rocks, nuggets and ore samples. You may reject gold if greater discrimination is used. Even the "zero" setting on non-calibrated detectors can result in rejected nuggets and ore. Consequently, always hunt in the All Metal mode. You'll also get more depth!

Because non-motion detectors are very sensitive to even small pieces of iron, you may find yourself digging extremely deep holes for bits and pieces of iron when operating in the All Metal mode. Be prepared!

When coin hunting, you can use discrimination to remove most of the problem, but when you are hunting for caches, you don't want to use any amount of discrimination, yet you hate to be bothered by detection of small, deeply buried targets. For more efficiency as well as depth when hunting large caches you should consider using the Depth Multiplier "two-box" attachment which ignores small metal pieces. These handy accessories are discussed more fully elsewhere in this book, particularly in Chapter 9 when we discuss cache hunting in greater detail.

#   #   #

My editor likes to tell the story about a young schoolboy assigned to read and report on a book about aquatic amphibians. The lad's book report (in full) read:

"This book told more about frogs than I wanted to know."

Perhaps, in this chapter I have told you more about metal detectors than you wanted to know. If so, I'm sorry you didn't put down *Let's Talk Treasure Hunting* sooner. It was a mighty fine treasure hunting guide until this last "frog" chapter, wasn't it?

The simple fact of the matter is that you don't need all of this detector knowledge with modern instruments. Just push one touchpad and begin finding treasure! It's that simple.

So, why don't we go treasure hunting together some day? Until then, I'll just hope for the chance to...

See you in the field!

Form for Ordering...

Ram Books
Gold Panning Kit

Please send the following books:

☐ Let's Talk Treasure Hunting $14.95
☐ Buried Treasures You Can Find $14.95
☐ Modern Metal Detectors $14.95
☐ Treasure Recovery from Sand & Sea $14.95
☐ Sunken Treasure: How to Find It $14.95
☐ Treasure from British Waters . . . . $ 7.95
☐ The New Successful Coin Hunting $12.95
☐ Modern Electronic Prospecting . . . . $ 9.95
☐ Weekend Prospecting . . . . $ 3.95
☐ Gold Panning Is Easy . . . . $ 9.95
☐ An Introduction to Metal Detectors . . . . . $ 1.00
  (No shipping/handling charge)
☐ Find an Ounce of Gold a Day . . . . $ 3.00
  (Included free with Gold Panning Kit)

True Treasure Tales

☐ Secret of John Murrell's Vault . . . . $ 4.95
☐ Missing Nez Perce Gold . . . . $ 4.95

Gold Panning Kit

☐ Complete kit for gold panning $24.95

  (Kit requires NO shipping/handling charge.)
  Also, when Gold Panning Kit is ordered,
  no shipping/handling charge for any books or videos.

Ram Publishing Company
P.O. Drawer 38649
Dallas, TX 75238
FAX: 214-494-1881
(Credit Card Orders Only)

Please add $1 for
each book
(maximum of $3
    handling charges.)

Total for items $_____

8.25% Tax (Texas residents) $_____

Handling Charge $_____

              TOTAL $_____

    Enclosed check or money order

    I prefer to order through
☐   MasterCard
☐   Visa
By telephone:
1-800-527-4011   _____
                      Credit Card Number

_____

Expiration Date   **Phone Number (8 a.m. to 4 p.m.)**

_____

Signature (Credit Card orders must be signed.)

_____

NAME

_____

ADDRESS (For Shipping)

_____

CITY, STATE, ZIP